Regulated F

Regulated Hatred

and other essays on Jane Austen

by
D.W. HARDING

Edited by
Monica Lawlor

THE ATHLONE PRESS
London & Atlantic Highlands, NJ

First published 1998 by
THE ATHLONE PRESS
1 Park Drive, London NW11 7SG
and 165 First Avenue,
Atlantic Highlands, NJ 07716

British Library Cataloguing in Publication Data
*A Catalogue record for this book is available
from the British Library*

ISBN 0 485 11522 0 hb
ISBN 0 485 12136 0 pb

Library of Congress Cataloging-in-Publication Data

Harding, Denys Clement Wyatt, 1908–
    Regulated hatred and other essays on Jane Austen / by D. W. Harding
; edited by Monica Lawlor.
        p.   cm.
    Includes bibliographical references and index.
    ISBN 0–485–11522–0 (hb). — ISBN 0–485–12136–0 (pb)
    1. Austen, Jane, 1775–1817—Criticism and interpretation.
    2. Women and literature—England—History—19th century.   I. Title.
PR4037.H29   1998
823′.7—dc21   98–2524
                                                                              CIP

Typeset by Ensystems, Saffron Walden

Printed and bound in Great Britain by
Cambridge University Press

Contents

Preface

The essays in this collection were selected as the best of
D.W. Harding's writing about his favourite author. A
number of the essays were published in the author's
lifetime, but the remainder were in manuscript form when
he died. Some editing of the manuscript material was
required, but nothing of substance has been altered or
added. The essays were written over a period of nearly 60
years; for this reason a brief chronology of the author has
been appended, so that the reader has the opportunity to
place the ideas in their biographical context. The foreword
by D.W. Harding's close friend, the late L.C. Knights,
provides a fuller account of the literary world in which
the essays were written.

The manuscripts of the unpublished work are now in
the possession of Emmanuel College, Cambridge, together
with the rest of the Harding archive which was given to
the College by his nephew, Martin Dilly.

M.M.L.

Foreword

It may help to define the nature of Harding's distinction as a critic if I recall a remark he once made, that it was his great good fortune, when at Cambridge, to have been taught by F.R. Leavis when reading English, and by R.W. Pickford when he switched to Psychology. (He got a First in both subjects.) Leavis, who never tired of showing how works of literature, if read with full personal attention, could express an infinite range of human experience and human values: and Pickford who demonstrated with a rigour of a quite different kind a discipline where it is a condition of insight and understanding that the observer should be as far as possible detached from what he observes. Harding's criticism shows the marks of both disciplines.

A further personal note seems necessary. What his friends valued was the unusual quality of attention they received from him. I don't mean that he was invasive or that he was in the least like the cat in Stevie Smith's poem who loved to gallop about doing good: it was simply that if you expressed an interest or a problem to him you were sure of his full attention. His letters to his friends, even into old age, were things to be looked forward to and treasured.*

As a critic of poetry he was one of the most sanely subtle (or subtly sane) of his generation – witness his pioneering review of 'Burnt Norton' when it first

---

* I understand that there are collections of his letters, to quite different people, in various parts of the world.

appeared in Eliot's *Poems 1918–35*, and his continuing attention to Eliot's poetry, the more telling because it comes, admiringly from a standpoint far removed from the poet's religious beliefs and social attitudes. Almost all the work collected in his *Experience into Words* bears an alert re-telling long after its original publication. There is very little criticism in this field that so prompts fruitful enquiry.

He was an eager and life-long reader of novels. Here again, in considering his criticism, it seems necessary to link the personal with the formal. His approach to the novel is best indicated by a few lines from his little book, *Social Psychology and Individual Values*, where he writes of:

> the fact that we are – and probably are by nature – social beings and that we like other people; their satisfaction and happiness are of direct value to us, and acts of ours that spoil them conflict with one of the strongest systems of sentiment that we possess. The vast implications of this simple fact that most of us like other people has often been strangely neglected in discussion or moral behaviour.

There is nothing here that could incline us to sentimentality – Harding could be tart as well as sympathetic – but when he writes of novels it is human behaviour as it affects other people that is at the focus of attention. The invitation of the novel is to considered experience, considered that is in terms of a lively mind – say that of Henry James or Jane Austen – that can embody, and ask us to consider, varieties of significant human behaviour. He and his wife had what can only be called a life-long love affair with Jane Austen: 'Regulated Hatred', which decisively altered the course of Austen criticism, appeared in *Scrutiny* in 1940, and he was still working on her novels at the time of his death. I have spoken of him as a moralist, and so, in an unavoidable sense, he was. But mind and heart went together; and no one who reads these papers (not finally revised, and so with repetitions that the editors have been unable to iron out completely) can doubt that for him, as for Blake, 'Enjoyment' was 'the food of Intellect'.

One of Harding's favourite authors was Montaigne, and no one who reads his work in its whole range – which is very wide indeed – can doubt the family resemblance. What marks his criticism is the unfailing interest in human experience – its vagaries and its often unnoticed common forms. And I think he communicated this delight to his readers, which is more than can be said of most of us who set up as critics of literature.

L.C. Knights

CHAPTER 1

Regulated hatred:
An Aspect of the Work of Jane Austen

The impression of Jane Austen which has filtered through to the reading public, down from the first-hand critics, through histories of literature, university courses, literary journalism and polite allusion, deters many who might be her best readers from bothering with her at all. How can this popular impression be described? In my experience the first idea to be absorbed from the atmosphere surrounding her work was that she offered exceptionally favourable openings to the exponents of urbanity. Gentlemen of an older generation than mine spoke of their intention of re-reading her on their deathbeds; Eric Linklater's cultured Prime Minister in *The Impregnable Women* passes from surreptitious to abandoned reading of her novels as a national crisis deepens. With this there also came the impression that she provided a refuge for the sensitive when the contemporary world grew too much for them. So Beatrice Kean Seymour writes (*Jane Austen*): 'In a society which has enthroned the machine-gun and carried it aloft even into the quiet heavens, there will always be men and women – Escapist or not, as you please – who will turn to her novels with an unending sense of relief and thankfulness.'

I was given to understand that her scope was of course extremely restricted, but that within her limits she succeeded admirably in expressing the gentler virtues of a civilized social order. She could do this because she lived at a time when, as a sensitive person of culture, she could still feel that she had a place in society and could address the reading public as sympathetic equals; she might introduce unpleasant people into her stories but she could confidently expose them to a public opinion that condemned them. Chiefly, so I gathered, she was a delicate satirist, revealing with inimitable lightness of touch the comic foibles and amiable weaknesses of the people whom she lived amongst and liked.

All this was enough to make me quite certain I didn't want to read her. And it is, I believe, a seriously misleading impression. Fragments of the truth have been incorporated in it but they are fitted into a pattern whose total effect is false. And yet the wide currency of this false impression is an indication of Jane Austen's success in an essential part of her complex intention as a writer: her books are, as she meant them to be, read and enjoyed by precisely the sort of people whom she disliked; she is a literary classic of the society which attitudes like hers, held widely enough, would undermine.

In order to enjoy her books without disturbance those who retain the conventional notion of her work must always have had slightly to misread what she wrote at a number of scattered points, points where she took good care (not wittingly perhaps) that the misreading should be the easiest thing in the world. Unexpected astringencies occur which the comfortable reader probably overlooks, or else passes by as slight imperfections, trifling errors of tone brought about by a faulty choice of words. Look at the passage in *Northanger Abbey* where Henry Tilney offers a solemn reprimand of Catherine's fantastic suspicions about his father:

Dear Miss Morland, consider the dreadful nature of these suspicions you have entertained. What have you been judging from? Remember the country and the age in which we live. Remember that we are English,

that we are Christians. Consult your own understanding, your own sense of the probable, your own observation of what is passing around you. Does our
education prepare us for such atrocities? Do our laws
connive at them? Could they be perpetrated without
being known, in a country like this, where social and
literary intercourse is on such a footing, and where
roads and newspapers lay everything open?

Had the passage really been as I quote it nothing would
have been out of tone. But I omitted a clause. The last
sentence actually runs: 'Could they be perpetrated without
being known, in a country like this, where social and
literary intercourse is on such a footing, where every man
is surrounded by a neighbourhood of voluntary spies, and
where roads and newspapers lay everything open?' 'Where
every man is surrounded by a neighbourhood of voluntary
spies' – with its touch of paranoia that surprising remark is
badly out of tune both with 'Henry's astonishing generosity and nobleness of conduct' and with the accepted idea
of Jane Austen.

Yet it comes quite understandably from someone of
Jane Austen's sensitive intelligence, living in her world of
news and gossip interchanged amongst and around a large
family. She writes to Cassandra (14 September 1804), 'My
mother is at this moment reading a letter from my aunt.
Yours to Miss Irvine of which she had had the perusal
(which by the bye in your place I should not like) has
thrown them into a quandary about Charles and his
prospects. The case is that my mother had previously told
my aunt, without restriction, that . . . whereas you had
replied to Miss Irvine's inquiries on the subject with less
explicitness and more caution. Never mind, let them
puzzle on together.' And when Fanny Knight (her niece)
writes confidentially about her love affair, Jane Austen
describes ruses she adopted to avoid having to read the

letter to the family, and later implores Fanny to 'write *something* that may do to be read or told' (30 November 1814).

Why is it that, holding the view she did of people's spying, Jane Austen should slip it in amongst Henry Tilney's eulogies of the age? By doing so she achieves two ends, ends which she may not have consciously aimed at. In such a speech from such a character the remark is unexpected and unbelievable, with the result that it is quite unlikely to be taken in at all by many readers; it slips through their minds without creating a disturbance. It gets said, but with the minimum risk of setting people's backs up. The second end achieved by giving the remark such a context is that of off-setting it at once by more appreciative views of society and so refraining from indulging an exaggerated bitterness. The eulogy of the age is not nullified by the bitter clause, but neither can it wipe out the impression the clause makes on those who attend to it.

One cannot say that here the two attitudes modify one another. The technique is too weak. Jane Austen can bring both attitudes into the picture but she had not at this point made one picture of them. In *Persuasion* she does something of the same kind more delicately. Miss Elliot's chagrin at having failed to marry her cousin is being described in the terms of ordinary satire which invites the reading public to feel superior to Miss Elliot:

There was not a baronet from A to Z whom her feelings could have so willingly acknowledged as an equal. Yet so miserably had he conducted himself, that though she was at this present time (the summer of 1814) wearing black ribbons for his wife, she could not admit him to be worth thinking of again. The disgrace of his first marriage might, perhaps, as there was no reason to suppose it perpetuated by offspring, have been got over, had he not done worse;

At this point the satire suddenly directs itself against the public instead of Miss Elliot:

> but he had, as by the accustomary intervention of kind friends they had been informed, spoken most disrespectfully of them all .

In *Emma* the same thing is done still more effectively. Again Jane Austen seems to be on perfectly good terms with the public she is addressing and to have no reserve in offering the funniness and virtues of Mr Woodhouse and Miss Bates to be judged by the accepted standards of the public. She invites her readers to be just their natural patronizing selves. But this public that Jane Austen seems on such good terms with has some curious things said about it, not criticisms, but small notes of fact that are usually not made. They almost certainly go unnoticed by many readers, for they involve only the faintest change of tone from something much more usual and acceptable. When she says that Miss Bates 'enjoyed a most uncommon degree of popularity for a woman neither young, handsome, rich, nor married', this is fairly conventional satire that any reading public would cheerfully admit in its satirist and chuckle over. But the next sentence must have to be mentally re-written by the greater number of Jane Austen's readers. For them it probably runs, 'Miss Bates stood in the very worst predicament in the world having much of the public favour; and she had no intellectual superiority to make atonement to herself, or compel an outward respect from those who might despise her.' This, I suggest, is how most readers, lulled and disarmed by the amiable context, will soften what in fact reads, 'and she had no intellectual superiority to make atonement to herself, or frighten those who might hate her into outward respect'. Jane Austen was herself at this time 'neither young, handsome, rich, nor married', and the passage perhaps hints at the functions which her unquestioned intellectual superiority may have had for her.

This eruption of fear and hatred into the relationships of everyday social life is something that the urbane admirer of Jane Austen finds distasteful; it is not the satire of one who writes securely for the entertainment of her civilized acquaintances. And it has the effect, for the attentive reader, of changing the flavour of the more ordinary satire amongst which it is embedded.

Emma is especially interesting from this point or view. What is sometimes called its greater 'mellowness' largely consists in saying quietly and undisguisedly things which in the earlier books were put more loudly but in the innocuous form of caricature. Take conversation for instance. Its importance and its high (though by no means supreme) social value are of course implicit in Jane Austen's writings. But one should beware of supposing that a mind like hers therefore found the ordinary social intercourse of the period congenial and satisfying. In *Pride and Prejudice* she offers an entertaining caricature of card-table conversation at Lady Catherine de Bourgh's house.

> Their table was superlatively stupid. Scarcely a syllable was uttered that did not relate to the game, except when Mrs Jenkinson expressed her fears of Miss de Bourgh's being too hot or too cold, or having too much or too little light. A great deal more passed at the other table. Lady Catherine was generally speaking – stating the mistakes of the three others, or relating some anecdote of herself. Mr Collins was employed in agreeing to everything her ladyship said, thanking her for

every fish he won, and apologising if he thought he won too many. Sir William did not say much. He was storing his memory with anecdotes and noble names.

This invites the carefree enjoyment of all her readers. They can all feel superior to Lady Catherine and Mr Collins. But in *Emma* the style changes: the talk at the Cole's dinner party, a pleasant dinner party which the heroine enjoyed, is described as 'the usual rate of conversation; a few clever things said, a few downright silly, but by much the larger proportion neither the one nor the other – nothing worse than everyday remarks, dull repetitions, old news, and heavy jokes'. 'Nothing worse'! – that phrase is typical. It is not mere sarcasm by any means. Jane Austen genuinely valued the achievements of the civilization she lived within and never lost sight of the fact that there might be something vastly worse than the conversation she referred to. 'Nothing worse' is a positive tribute to the decency, the superficial friendliness, the absence of the grosser forms of insolence and self-display at the dinner party. At least Mrs Elton wasn't there. And yet the effect of the comment, if her readers took it seriously would be that of a disintegrating attack upon the sort of social intercourse they have established for themselves. It is not the comment of one who would have helped to make her society what it was, or ours what it is.

To speak of this aspect of her work as 'satire' is perhaps misleading. She has none of the underlying didactic intention ordinarily attributed to the satirist. Her object is not missionary; it is the more desperate one of merely finding some mode of existence for her critical attitudes. To her the first necessity was to keep on reasonably good terms with the associates of her everyday life; she had a deep need for their affection and a genuine respect for the ordered, decent civilization that they upheld. And yet she was sensitive to their crudenesses and complacencies and knew that her real existence depended on resisting many of the values they implied. The novels gave her a way out of this dilemma. This, rather than the ambition of entertaining a posterity of urbane gentlemen, was her motive force in writing.

As a novelist, therefore, part of her aim was to find the means for unobtrusive spiritual survival, without open conflict with the friendly people around her whose standards in simpler things she could accept and whose affection she greatly needed. She found, of course, that one of the most useful peculiarities of her society was its willingness to remain blind to the implications of a caricature. She found people eager to laugh at faults they tolerated in themselves and their friends, so long as the faults were exaggerated and the laughter 'good-natured' – so long, that is, as the assault on society could be regarded as a mock assault and not genuinely disruptive. Satire such as this is obviously a means not of admonition but of self-preservation.

Hence one of Jane Austen's most successful methods is to offer her readers every excuse for regarding as rather exaggerated figures of fun people whom she herself detests and fears. Mrs Bennet, according to the Austen tradition, is one of 'our' richly comic characters about whom we can feel superior, condescending, perhaps a trifle sympathetic, and above all heartily amused and free from care. Everything conspires to make this the natural interpretation once you are willing to overlook Jane Austen's bald and brief statement of her own attitude to her: 'She was a woman of mean understanding, little information, and uncertain temper.' How many women among Jane Austen's acquaintance and amongst her most complacent readers to the present day that phrase must describe! How gladly they enjoy the funny side of the situations Mrs Bennet's unpleasant nature creates, and how easy it is made for them to forget or never observe that Jane Austen, none the less for seeing how funny she is, goes on detesting her. The thesis that the ruling standards of our social group leave a perfectly comfortable niche for detestable people and give them sufficient sanction to persist, would, if it were argued seriously, arouse the most violent opposition, the most determined apologetics for things as they are, and the most reproachful pleas for a sense of proportion.

Caricature served Jane Austen's purpose perfectly. Under her treatment one can never say where caricature leaves off and the claim to serious portraiture begins. Mr Collins is only given a trifle more comic exaggeration than Lady Catherine de Bourgh, and by her standards is a possible human being. Lady Catherine in turn seems acceptable as a portrait if the criterion of verisimilitude is her nephew Mr Darcy. And he, finally, although to some extent a caricature, is near enough natural portraiture to stand beside Elizabeth Bennet, who, like all the heroines, is presented as an undistorted portrait. The simplest comic effects are gained by bringing the caricatures into direct contact with the real people, as in Mr Collins' visit to the Bennets and his proposal to Elizabeth. But at the same time one knows that, though some easy points of view caricature, in other directions he does, by easy stages, fit into the real world. He is real enough to Mrs Bennet; and she is real enough to Elizabeth to create a situation of real misery for her when she refuses. Consequently the proposal scene is not only comic fantasy, but it is also, for Elizabeth, a taste of the fantastic nightmare in which economic and social institutions have such power over the values of personal relationships that the comic monster is nearly able to get her.

The implications of her caricatures as criticism of real people in real society is brought out in the way they dovetail into their social setting. The decent, stodgy Charlotte puts up cheerfully with Mr Collins as a husband; and Elizabeth can never quite become reconciled to the idea that her friend is the wife of her comic monster. And that, of course, is precisely the sort of idea that Jane Austen herself could never grow reconciled to. The people she hated were tolerated, accepted, comfortably ensconced in the only human society she knew; they were, for her, society's embarrassing unconscious comment on itself. A recent writer on Jane Austen, Elizabeth Jenkins, puts forward the polite and more comfortable interpretation in supposing Charlotte's marriage to be explained solely by the impossibility of young women's earning their own living at that period. But Charlotte's complaisance goes deeper than that: it is shown as a considered indifference to personal relationships when they conflict with cruder advantages in the wider social world:

> She had always felt that Charlotte's opinion of matrimony was not exactly like her own, but she could not have supposed it possible that, when called into action, she would have sacrificed every better feeling to worldly advantage.

We know too, at the biographical level, that Jane Austen herself, in a precisely similar situation to Charlotte's, spent a night of psychological crisis in deciding to revoke her acceptance of an 'advantageous' proposal made the previous evening. And her letters to Fanny Knight show how deep her convictions went at this point.

It is important to notice that Elizabeth makes no break with her friend on account of the marriage. This was the sort of friend – 'a friend disgracing herself and sunk in her esteem' – that went to make up the available social world which one could neither escape materially nor be independent of psychologically. The impossibility of being cut off from objectionable people is suggested more subtly in *Emma*, where Mrs Elton is the high light of the pervasive neglect of spiritual values in social life. One can hardly doubt that Jane Austen's own dealings with society are reflected in the passage where Mr Weston makes the error of inviting Mrs Elton to join the picnic party which he and Emma have planned:

> Emma could not but feel some surprise, and a little displeasure, on hearing from Mr Weston that he had been proposing to Mrs Elton, as her brother and sister had failed her, that the two parties should unite, and go together, and that as Mrs Elton had very readily acceded to it, so it was to be, if she had no objection. Now, as her objection was nothing but her very great dislike of Mrs Elton, of which Mr Weston must already be perfectly aware, it was not worth bringing forward; it could not be done without a reproof to him, which would be giving pain to his wife; and she found herself, therefore, obliged to consent to an arrangement which she would have done a great deal to avoid; an arrangement which would, probably, expose her even to the degradation of being said to be of Mrs Elton's party! Every feeling was offended; and the forbearance of her outward submission left a heavy arrear due to secret severity in her reflections, on the unmanageable goodwill of Mr Weston's temper.
>
> 'I am glad you approve of what I have done,' said he, very comfortably. 'But I thought you would. Such schemes as these are nothing without numbers. One cannot have too large a party. A large party secures its own amusement. And she is a good-natured woman after all. One could not leave her out.'
>
> Emma denied none of it aloud, and agreed to none of it in private.

This well illustrates Jane Austen's typical dilemma: of being intensely critical of people to whom she also has strong emotional attachments.

The social group having such ambivalence for her, it is not surprising if her conflict should find some outlets not fully within her conscious control. To draw attention to these, however, is not to suggest that they lessen the value of her conscious intention and its achievements.

The chief instance is the fascination she found in the Cinderella theme, the Cinderella theme with the fairy godmother omitted. For in Jane Austen's treatment the natural order of things manages to reassert the heroine's proper pre-eminence without the intervention of any human or quasi-human helper. In this respect she allies the Cinderella theme to another fairy-tale theme which is often introduced – that of the princess brought up by unworthy parents but never losing the delicate sensibilities which are an inborn part of her. This latter theme appears most explicitly in *Mansfield Park*, the unfinished story of *The Watsons*, and, with some softening, in *Pride and Prejudice*. The contrast between Fanny Price's true nature and her squalid home at Portsmouth is the clearest statement of the idea, but in the first four of the finished novels the heroine's final position is, even in the worldly sense, always above her reasonable social expectations by conventional standards, but corresponding to her natural worth.

To leave it at this, however, would be highly misleading. It is the development which occurs in her treatment of the Cinderella theme that most rewards attention. In *Northanger Abbey, Sense and Sensibility* and *Pride and Prejudice* it is handled simply; the heroine is in some degree isolated from those around her by being more sensitive or of finer moral insight or sounder judgment, and her marriage to the handsome prince at the end is in the nature of a reward for being different from the rest and a consolation for the distresses entailed by being different. This is true even of *Northanger Abbey* in spite of the grotesque error of judgment that Catherine Morland is guilty of and has to renounce. For here Jane Austen was interested not so much in the defect in her heroine's judgment as in the absurdly wide currency of the 'gothick' tradition that entrapped her. Catherine throws off her delusion almost as something external to herself. And this is so glaring that Jane Austen seems to have been uncomfortable about it: in describing it she resorts to a rather factitious semi-detachment from her heroine.

> Her mind made up on these several points, and her resolution formed, of always judging and acting in future with the greatest good sense, and had nothing to do but to forgive herself and be happier than ever; and the lenient hand of time did much for her by insensible gradations in the course of another day.

In *Sense and Sensibility* and *Pride and Prejudice* the heroines are still nearer perfection and even the handsome princes have faults to overcome before all is well. Immediately after her final reconciliation with Mr Darcy, Elizabeth Bennet is tempted to laugh at his over-confident direction of his friend Bingley's love affair, 'but she checked herself. She remembered that he had yet to learn to be laughed at, and it was rather too early to begin.'

To put the point in general terms, the heroine of these early novels is herself the criterion of sound judgment and good feeling. She may claim that her values are sanctioned by good breeding and a religious civilization, but in fact none of the people she meets represents those values so effectively as she does herself. She is never in submissive alliance with the representatives of virtue and good feeling in her social world – there is only a selective alliance with certain aspects of their characters. The social world may have material power over her, enough to make her unhappy, but it hasn't the power that comes from having created or moulded her, and it can claim no credit for her being what she is. In this sense the heroine is independent of those about her and isolated from them. She has only to be herself.

The successful handling of this kind of theme and this heroine brought Jane Austen to the point where a development became psychologically possible. The hint of irrationality underlying the earlier themes could be brought nearer the light. She could begin to admit that even a heroine must owe a great deal of her character and values to the social world in which she had been moulded, and, that being so, could hardly be quite so solitary in her excellence as the earlier heroines are. The emphasis hitherto has been almost entirely on the difference between the heroine and the people about her. But this was to slight the reality of her bond with the ordinary 'good' people; there was more to be said for the fundamentals of virtue and seemliness than she had been implying. And so, after the appearance of *Pride and Prejudice*, she wrote to Cassandra, 'Now I will try and write of something else, and it shall be a complete change of subject – ordination' (29 January 1813).

This sets the tone of *Mansfield Park*, the new novel. Here her emphasis is on the deep importance of the conventional virtues, of civilized seemliness, decorum and sound religious feeling. These become the worthy objects of the heroine's loyalties; and they so nearly comprise the whole range of her values that Fanny Price is the least interesting of all the heroines. For the first time, Jane Austen sets the heroine in submissive alliance with the conventionally virtuous people of the story, Sir Thomas and Edmund. Mistaken though these pillars of society may in some respects be, the heroine's proper place is at their side; their standards are worthy of a sensitive person's support and complete allegiance.

It is a novel in which Jane Austen pays tribute to the virtuous fundamentals of her upbringing, ranging herself with those whom she considers right on the simpler and more obvious moral issues, and withdrawing her attention – relatively at least – from the finer details of living in which they may disturb her. She allies herself with virtues that are easy to appreciate and reasonably often met with. The result, as one would expect, is a distinct tendency to priggishness. And, of course, the book was greatly liked. 'Mr H[aden] is reading *Mansfield Park* for the first time and prefers it to *P. and P.*' (26 November 1815). 'Mr Cook [himself a clergyman] says "it is the most sensible novel he ever read," and the manner in which I treat the clergy delights them very much.' (14 June 1814). Compared with *Mansfield Park*, Jane Austen is afraid that *Emma* will appear 'inferior in good sense' (11 December 1815). It was after reading *Mansfield Park*, moreover, that the pompously self-satisfied Librarian to the Prince Regent offered her, almost avowedly, his own life story as the basis for a novel about an English clergyman. He must have been one of the first of the admirer-victims who have continued to enjoy her work to this day. And her tactful and respectful reply ('The comic part of the character I might be equal to, but not the good, the enthusiastic, the literary') illustrates admirably her capacity for keeping on good terms with people without too great treachery to herself.

The priggishness of *Mansfield Park* is the inevitable result of the curiously abortive attempt at humility that the novel represents. Although it involves the recognition that heroines are not spontaneously generated but owe much of their personality to the established standards of their society, and perfection of the heroine is still not doubted. And so the effort towards humility becomes in effect the exclamation, 'Why, some of the very good people are nearly as good as I am and really do deserve my loyalty!'

There is no external evidence that Jane Austen was other than highly satisfied with *Mansfield Park*, which is,

after all, in many ways interesting and successful. But its
reductio ad absurdum of the Cinderella theme and the
foundling princess theme could hardly have been without
effect. This, I think, is already visible in the last chapter,
which, with its suggestion of a fairy-tale winding up of
the various threads of the story, is ironically perfunctory.
For instance:

> I purposely abstain from dates on this occasion, that
> every one may be at liberty to fix their own, aware that
> the cure of unconquerable passions, and the transfer of
> unchanging attachments, must vary much as to time in
> different people. I only entreat everybody to believe
> that exactly at the time when it was quite natural that it
> should be so, and not a week earlier, Edmund did cease
> to care about Miss Crawford, and became as anxious to
> marry Fanny as Fanny herself could desire.

And Sir Thomas's 'high sense of having realised a great
acquisition in the promise of Fanny for a daughter, formed
just such a contrast with his early opinion on the subject
when the poor little girl's coming had first been agitated,
as time is for ever producing between the plans and
decisions of mortals, for their own instruction and their
neighbours' entertainment'.

Whether or not Jane Austen realized what she had been
doing, at all events the production of *Mansfield Park*
enabled her to go on next to the extraordinary achievement of *Emma*, in which a much more complete humility
is combined with the earlier unblinking attention to
people as they are. The underlying argument has a
different trend. She continues to see that the heroine has
derived from the people and conditions around her, but
she now keeps clearly in mind the objectionable features
of those people; and she faces the far bolder conclusion
that even a heroine is likely to have assimilated many of

the more unpleasant possibilities of the human being in society. And it is not that society has spoilt an originally perfect girl who now has to recover her pristine good sense, as it was with Catherine Morland, but that the heroine has not yet achieved anything like perfection and is actually going to learn a number of serious lessons from some of the people she lives with.

Consider in the first place the treatment here of the two favourite themes of the earlier novels. The Cinderella theme is now relegated to the sub-heroine, Jane Fairfax. Its working out involves the discomfiture of the heroine, who in this respect is put into the position of one of the ugly sisters. Moreover the Cinderella procedure is shown in the light of a social anomaly, rather a nuisance and requiring the excuse of unusual circumstances.

The associated theme of the child brought up in humble circumstances whose inborn nature fits her for better things is frankly parodied and deflated in the story of Harriet Smith, the illegitimate child whom Emma tries to turn into a snob. In the end, with the insignificant girl cheerfully married to a deserving farmer, 'Harriet's parentage became known. She proved to be the daughter of a tradesman, rich enough to afford her the comfortable maintenance which had ever been hers, and decent enough to have always wished for concealment. Such was the blood of gentility which Emma had formerly been so ready to vouch for!'

Thus the structure of the narrative expresses a complete change in Jane Austen's outlook on the heroine in relation to others. And the story no longer progresses towards her vindication or consolation; it consists in her gradual, humbling self-enlightenment. Emma's personality includes some of the tendencies and qualities that Jane Austen most disliked – self-complacency, for instance, malicious enjoyment in prying into embarrassing private affairs, snobbery, and a weakness for meddling in other people's lives. But now, instead of being attributed in exaggerated form of a character distanced into caricature, they occur in the subtle form given them by someone who in many ways had admirably fine standards.

We cannot say that in *Emma* Jane Austen abandons the Cinderella story. She so deliberately inverts it that we ought to regard *Emma* as a bold variant of the theme and a further exploration of its underlying significance for her. In *Persuasion* she goes back to the Cinderella situation in its most direct and simple form, but develops a vitally important aspect of it that she had previously avoided. This is the significance for Cinderella of her idealized dead mother.

Most children are likely to have some conflict of attitude towards their mother, finding her in some respects an ideal object of love and in others an obstacle to their wishes and a bitter disappointment. For a child such as Jane Austen who actually was in many ways more sensitive and able than her mother, one can understand that this conflict may persist in some form for a very long time. Now one of the obvious appeals of the Cinderella story, as of all stories of wicked stepmothers, is that it resolves the ambivalence of the mother by the simple plan of splitting her in two: the ideal mother is dead and can be adored without risk of disturbance; the living mother is completely detestable and can be hated whole-heartedly without self-reproach.*

In her early novels Jane Austen consistently avoided dealing with a mother who could be a genuinely intimate friend of her daughter. Lady Susan, of the unfinished novel, is her daughter's enemy. In *Northanger Abbey* the mother is busy with the household and the younger

---

* This is, needless to say, only a very small part of the unconscious significance which such stories may have for a reader. Most obviously it neglects the relationships of the stepmother and the heroine to the father.

children. In *Sense and Sensibility* she herself has to be
guided and kept in hand by her daughter's sounder
judgment. In *Pride and Prejudice* she is Mrs Bennet. In
Mansfield Park she is a slattern whom the heroine only
visits once in the course of the novel. In *Emma* the mother
is dead and Miss Taylor, her substitute, always remains to
some extent the promoted governess. This avoidance may
seem strange, but it can be understood as the precaution
of a mind which, although in the Cinderella situation, is
still too sensitive and honest to offer as a complete portrait
the half-truth of the idealized dead mother.

But in *Persuasion* she does approach the problem which
is latent here. She puts her heroine in the Cinderella
setting, and so heightens her need for affection. And then
in Lady Russell she provides a godmother, not fairy but
human, with whom Anne Elliot can have much the
relationship of a daughter with a greatly loved, but
humanly possible, mother. Jane Austen then goes on to
face the implications of such a relationship – and there
runs through the whole story a lament for seven years' loss
of happiness owing to Anne's having yielded to her
godmother's persuasion.

The novel opens with her being completely convinced
of the wrongness of the advice she received, and yet
strongly attached to Lady Russell still and unable to blame
her. Her attitude is, and throughout the book remains,
curiously unresolved. 'She did not blame Lady Russell,
she did not blame herself, for having been guided by her;
but she felt that were any young person in similar
circumstances to apply to her for counsel, they would
never receive any of such certain immediate wretchedness,
such uncertain future good.' But for all that the rest of the
book shows Anne repeatedly resisting fresh advice from
her godmother and being completely vindicated in the
upshot.

This might mean that Anne was a repetition of the

earlier heroines, detached by her good sense and sound principles from the inferior standards of those about her. That would be true of her relations with her father and eldest sister. But she had no such easy detachment from her godmother. Lady Russell was near enough to the ideal mother to secure Anne's affection, to make her long for the comfort of yielding to her judgment. This satisfaction – the secure submission to a parent who seems completely adequate – was denied Anne by her superior judgment. She was strong enough to retain the insight that separated her from Lady Russell – they never mentioned the episode in the years that followed and neither knew what the other felt about it – but she never came to feel her partial detachment from her as anything but a loss. Nor could she ever regret having yielded to Lady Russell's advice, even though she regretted that the advice had been so mistaken. At the end of the story, reverting to the old dilemma, she tells the lover whom she has now regained:

> I have been thinking over the past, and trying to judge of the right and wrong – I mean with regard to myself; and I must believe that I was right, much as I suffered from it – that I was perfectly right in being guided by the friend whom you will love better than you do now. To me, she was in the place of a parent. Do not mistake me, however. I am not saying that she did not err in her service. It was, perhaps, one of those cases in which advice is good or bad only as the event decides and for myself, I certainly never should, in any circumstances of tolerable similarity, give such advice. But I mean that I was right in submitting to her, and that if I had done otherwise, I should have suffered more in continuing the engagement than I did even in giving it up, because I should have suffered in my conscience.

It is in *Persuasion* that Jane Austen fingers what is probably the tenderest spot for those who identify themselves with Cinderella: she brings the idealized mother back to life and admits that she is no nearer to perfection than the mothers of acute and sensitive children generally are.

This attempt to suggest a slightly different emphasis in the reading of Jane Austen is not offered as a balanced appraisal of her work. It is deliberately lop-sided, neglecting the many points at which the established view seems adequate. I have tried to underline one or two features of her work that claim the sort of readers who sometimes miss her – those who would turn to her not for relief and escape but as a formidable ally against things and people which were to her, and still are, hateful.

ADDENDUM

Mansfield Park and 'Ordination'

Editorial note: What follows is part of a letter in which D.W.H. sets out his reason for revising the opinion expressed on this issue in the forgoing paper. He noted elsewhere that if the 1940 paper was to be reprinted this 'error' must be corrected; in accordance with the spirit of that note the relevant part of the letter is appended here.

Dr R.W. Chapman has pointed out (*Facts and Problems*) that it is difficult to understand the letter (29 January 1813) in which Jane Austen tells Cassandra, after describing the publication of *Pride and Prejudice*, that she will now try to write of something else, and it shall be ordination. Like many people, I had at first taken it to indicate her intention to embark on *Mansfield Park*. But in fact she had already written more than half of it and Cassandra had read the draft, as Dr Chapman shows. None the less, in indexing the *Letters* he implies that the 'change' is from the subject-matter of *Pride and Prejudice* to the subject-matter of *Mansfield Park*. I think now that the sentence has been misapplied. It refers not to her novel writing but to what she is writing in this very letter. She has written about the publication of *Pride and Prejudice* at which is for her great length, taking up half the letter on a topic that might seem egotistical. She breaks off abruptly with what amounts to a tacit apology, and I take it that in reading the sentence we should emphasize 'will': 'Now I will try to write of something else, & it shall be a complete change of subject – ordination – I am glad to find your enquiries have ended so well.' We know from the previous letter that at this time she had got at least as far as Volume II, Chapter VII in *Mansfield Park*. In Chapter VIII she goes on to deal with Edmund's decision to stay with a friend near Peterborough and 'receive ordination in the course of the Christmas week'. She had evidently asked Cassandra, who was visiting James, their clergyman brother, to settle some point connected with ordination. Dr Chapman supposes that the enquiries may have been about the disposal of livings, but from the punctuation it seems likelier that ordination was the subject. And it was the subject of Jane Austen's new departure in her letter, not the subject of *Mansfield Park*.

CHAPTER 2

Family Life in the Eighteenth
and Early Nineteenth Centuries

The crucial importance of a family's social position to its
individual members in eighteenth and nineteenth century
England could not fail to be recorded in the work of a
novelist so steeped in her own everyday reality, and since
she was living in a period of rather rapid change in the
class system, the consequent uncertainties are also
reflected. The Austens belonged to the gentry, the very
broad division of English society that nominally excluded
anyone engaged in trade and extended upward until it
reached the boundary line with the nobility, ranging
therefore from the baronet, with the highest rank among
the gentry, down to the daughter of a man with a small
landed estate or a clergyman with a living (though a
curate, to judge by Sir Walter Elliot's standards, was not a
gentleman). Economically the daughter of a gentleman
was entirely dependent on her family, unless it was so
poor that she was reduced to supporting herself as a
governess. Both her dowry and her connections would
influence her chance of marriage: Mr Wickham and Mr
Elton had an eye to the money their wives would bring
them and Mr Weston was thought to have made an
amazingly good match in his first marriage by connecting
himself with the Churchills. If gentlewomen were left
with reduced means their comfort would depend partly
on the help given by members of the extended family –
and so, when Mrs Dashwood and her daughters are failed
by the meanness of Mr John Dashwood it is a cousin of

hers who offers them Barton Cottage at a low rent and helps them to live in moderate comfort.

Although marriage was so openly seen as an economic arrangement and a means of alliance between families involving a bargain in terms of money and prestige, the possibility that these material calculations might be upset by the irrationalities of love was an equally important social fact, and the hazards of marriage, especially the girl's good or bad luck, are at least as prominent in the novels as they could have been in reality. The conception of *Mansfield Park* is bound up intimately with the obligations that unite an extended family even when differences of marriage have put great social and economic distances between its members. The whole situation is condensed in the opening paragraph:

> About thirty years ago, Miss Maria Ward of Hunting-don, with only seven thousand pounds, had the good luck to captivate Sir Thomas Bertram, of Mansfield Park, in the county of Northampton, and to be thereby raised to the rank of a baronet's lady, with all the comforts and consequences of a handsome house and large income. All Huntingdon exclaimed on the great-ness of the match, and her uncle, the lawyer, himself, allowed her to be at least three thousand pounds short of any equitable claim to it. She had two sisters to be benefited by her elevation; and such of their acquaint-ance who thought Miss Ward and Miss Frances quite as handsome as Miss Maria, did not scruple to predict their marrying with almost equal advantage. But there are certainly not so many men of large fortune in the world, as there are pretty women to deserve them. Miss Ward, at the end of half a dozen years, found herself obliged to be attached to the Rev. Mr Norris, a friend of her brother-in-law, with scarcely any private fortune, and Miss Frances fared yet worse. Miss Ward's match,

indeed, when it comes to the point, was not contemptible, Sir Thomas being happily able to give his friend an
income in the living of Mansfield, and Mr and Mrs
Norris began their career of conjugal felicity with very
little less than a thousand a year. But Miss Frances
married, in the common phrase, to disoblige her family,
and by fixing on a Lieutenant of Marines, without
education, fortune, or connections, did it very thoroughly. She could hardly have made a more untoward
choice. Sir Thomas Bertram had interest, which, from
principle as well as pride, from a general wish of doing
right, and a desire of seeing all that were connected
with him in situations of respectability, he would have
been glad to exert for the advantage of Lady Bertram's
sister; but her husband's profession was such as no
interest could reach.

The breach between Mrs Price and her more fortunate
sisters is promptly healed when she pleads for forgiveness
and help, and although it was Mrs Norris who had opened
the breach by her long and angry letter to her sister it is
also Mrs Norris who now connects the families by getting
Fanny Price to Mansfield Park. The novel takes its title
from the estate, and the estate is the centre of the family
with all its ties and influences. The network includes the
Prices, the Rushworths with whom an alliance is arranged
through Maria's loveless marriage, the Grants in the
rectory, with the Crawfords to whom they are related,
and then the Crawfords' uncle, the Admiral through
whose influence William Price is promoted. Such a family
formed a nodal point in the community and had obligations to it. Faced with Mrs Norris's demand that Maria
should be received at home in spite of her adultery, Sir
Thomas assured her that 'had there been no young person
of either sex belonging to him, to be endangered by the
society, or hurt by the character of Mrs Rushworth, he

would never have offered so great an insult to the
neighbourhood, as to expect it to notice her'. Such an
attitude, expressed in the banishment of Maria, made at
least for respectability and decorum.

Some of the limitations of the family as a psychological
matrix and as a social institution, however, are made
unmistakably clear in the failure of Maria's and Julia's
upbringing, in the substitution of rules of propriety for
deeper principles of conduct and in the failure of Sir
Thomas to make a personal relation with his daughters
and secure their real affection. Without this the family
that provided such security could be experienced as a
prison, as Maria indicates in the symbolic episode of her
escaping without Mr Rushworth's permission from the
bounds of his little wood, when Mr Crawford's later
seduction of her is figuratively and punningly enacted. He
reminds her of her engagement and prospects:

'You have a very smiling scene before you.'

'Do you mean literally or figuratively? Literally I
conclude. Yes, certainly, the sun shines and the park
looks very cheerful. But unluckily that iron gate, that
ha-ha, give me a feeling of restraint and hardship. I
cannot get out, as the starling said.' As she spoke, and it
was with expression, she walked to the gate; he followed her. 'Mr Rushworth is so long fetching this key!'

'And for the world you would not get out without
the key and without Mr Rushworth's authority and
protection, or I think you might with little difficulty
pass round the edge of the gate, here, with my assistance; I think it might be done, if you really wished to
be more at large, and could allow yourself to think it
not prohibited.'

'Prohibited! nonsense. I certainly can get out that
way, and I will.'

Fanny, feeling all this to be wrong, could not help making an effort to prevent it. 'You will hurt yourself, Miss Bertram,' she cried, 'you will certainly hurt yourself against those spikes – you will tear your gown – you will be in danger of slipping into the ha-ha.'

On this occasion Maria escaped the dangers, but when the literal seduction and elopement took place the penalties prefigured in Fanny's warning were fully exacted. Julia too resorted to her foolish elopement because she imagined that the certain consequence to herself of her sister's conduct 'would be greater severity and restraint'. For her as for Maria the family had aspects of a prison.

Both in its security and in its constraint it formed part of a neighbourhood. The mutual dependence of the local families for their entertainment is highlighted in the occasional balls and dinners and the parties of pleasure such as the one in *Sense and Sensitbility* which gets disturbed by Colonel Brandon's sudden departure for London. But the consequence of such closeness was also lack of privacy, with gossip fastening on everything it could, from Mrs Churchill's health to 'the situation of Mrs Weston, whose happiness it was to be hoped might eventually be as much increased by the arrival of a child, as that of all her neighbours was by the approach of it'. The misfortunes of the Bennets when Lydia's seduction by Wickham becomes known is heightened by the reaction of the neighbourhood. Jane mentions to Elizabeth that 'Lady Lucas has been very kind; she walked here on Wednesday morning to condole with us, and offered her services, or any of her daughters, if they could be of use to us.'

'She had better have stayed at home,' cried Elizabeth; 'perhaps she *meant* well, but, under such a misfortune as this, one cannot see too little of one's neighbours. Assistance is impossible; condolence, insufferable. Let them triumph over us at a distance, and be satisfied.'

And then, when Wickham was induced to marry Lydia:

> The good news quickly spread through the house, and with proportionate speed through the neighbourhood. It was borne in the latter with decent philosophy. To be sure it would have been more for the advantage of conversation, had Miss Lydia Bennet come upon the town; or, as the happiest alternative, been secluded from the world, in some distant farm house. But there was much to be talked of, in marrying her; and the good-natured wishes for her well-doing, which had proceeded before, from all the spiteful old ladies in Meryton, lost but little of their spirit in this change of circumstances, because with such an husband, her misery was considered certain.

It is understandable that Henry Tilney in *Northanger Abbey* speaks of 'a country like this . . . where every man is surrounded by a neighbourhood of voluntary spies.'

Not only spitefulness but friendly interest and well-meant officiousness produced the constraint of having all one's actions under observation. Mr John Knightley is kindly concerned that Jane Fairfax should have been out walking on a rainy morning; Mr Woodhouse, still more anxious, adds his inquiries and advice; news of the walk in the rain reaches Mrs Elton and on hearing that Jane has gone to get letters from the post office, she officiously insists that in future their servant shall collect Jane's letters each morning. And Jane has then to put up every possible resistance in order to safeguard her clandestine correspondence with Frank Churchill.

The closeness of the neighbourhood, itself almost like a

family, is vividly conveyed in Emma's reflections on the situation of Harriet, Mr Elton and herself after she has refused his proposal and revealed her belief that he was in love with Harriet. The distressing explanation she had to make to Harriet, and all that poor Harriet would be suffering, with the awkwardness of future meetings, the difficulties of continuing or discontinuing the acquaintance, of subduing feelings, concealing resentment, and avoiding éclat . . . but it seemed to her reasonable that at Harriet's age, and with the entire extinction of all hope, such a progress might be made towards a state of composure by the time of Mr Elton's return, as to allow them all to meet again in the common routine of acquaintance, without any danger of betraying sentiments or increasing them:

> Their being fixed, so absolutely fixed, in the same place, was bad for each, for all three. Not one of them had the power of removal, or of effecting any material change of society. They must encounter each other, and make the best of it.

Marriage, within the network of families, was inevitably seen in the light of the alliances and connections it brought, and not merely by the worldly characters whom Jane Austen implicitly condemns but by those she thinks well of. Mrs Croft, faced with the prospect that her brother may marry one of the Musgrove girls, remarks 'Very good humoured, unaffected girls, indeed, . . . and a very respectable family. One could not be connected with better people.' And when Emma Woodhouse visits Donwell Abbey and reminds herself of the details of the house and grounds, to which her sister's marriage connected her:

> She felt all the honest pride and complacency which her alliance with the present and future proprietor

could fairly warrant ... Some faults of temper John
Knightley had; but Isabella had connected herself unex-
ceptionably. She had given them neither men, nor
names, nor places, that could raise a blush.

On the other hand Jane Austen's values are such that it
is in the end the personal qualities of the people with
whom marriage brings connection that matter far more
than their social rank. Although family connections are at
first such a stumbling block for Elizabeth Bennet and Mr
Darcy, in the end after marriage they select among their
relations as individuals; it is, on Elizabeth's side, Mr
Bennet, the Gardiners and an improving Kitty who are
brought frequently to Pemberley, and on Darcy's side
only his sister Georgiana who is regularly there. So too
when Anne Elliot marries Captain Wentworth, although
it is she who brings the grander connections, Jane Austen
makes her feel acutely their inferiority as people to the
connections he brings her:

> Anne, satisfied at a very early period of Lady Russell's
> meaning to love Captain Wentworth as she ought, had
> no other alloy to the happiness of her prospects than
> what arose from the consciousness of having no relations
> to bestow on him which a man of sense could value.
> There she felt her own inferiority keenly. The dispro-
> portion in their fortune was nothing; it did not give her
> a moment's regret; but to have no family to receive and
> estimate him properly; nothing of respectability, of
> harmony, of good-will to offer in return for all the
> worth and all the prompt welcome which met her in
> his brothers and sisters, was a source of as lively pain
> as her mind could well be sensible of, under circum-
> stances of otherwise strong felicity. She had but two
> friends in the world to add to his list, Lady Russell and
> Mrs Smith.

This is a passage of very strong emphasis, considering that Anne's family had after all come to accept the match with more than mere resignation. It sweeps them all aside, and with them their connection with the nobility through 'our cousins, the Dalrymples'; she had 'no relations to bestow on him which a man of sense could value'.

On the economic realities of marriage also Jane Austen expresses, as the background of her characters' lives, the conventional outlook of her society, but equally she conveys her own more personal view of the problem. In *Sense and Sensibility* the conventional standpoint is treated with rather heavy satire in Mrs Ferrars's plans for marrying her elder son to Miss Morton, who is Lord Morton's daughter and possessed of £30,000. When the revelation of Edward's engagement to Lucy Steele puts that out of the question and Edward has been cast off by his mother in favour of his younger brother Robert, Elinor hears of the family's revised plans:

'We think *now*' – said Mr Dashwood, after a short pause, 'of *Robert's* marrying Miss Morton.'

Elinor, smiling at the grave and decisive importance of her brother's tone, calmly replied,

'The lady, I suppose has no choice in the affair.'

'Choice! – how do you mean?'

'I only mean, that I suppose from your manner of speaking, it must be the same to Miss Morton whether she marry Edward or Robert.'

'Certainly, there can be no difference; for Robert will now to all intents and purposes be considered as the eldest son; – and as to anything else, they are both very agreeable young men, I do not know that one is superior to the other.'

With the lighter touch that marks the style of *Pride and Prejudice*, the same aspect of marriage is treated in a less laboured way when Colonel Fitzwilliam, although attracted to Elizabeth, indicates that as an earl's younger son he cannot afford to contemplate a serious attachment to someone without money:

> 'Our habits of expence make us too dependant, and there are not many in my rank of life who can afford to marry without some attention to money.'
>
> 'Is this,' thought Elizabeth, 'meant for me?' and she coloured at the idea; but, recovering herself, said in a lively tone, 'And pray, what is the usual price of an Earl's younger son? Unless the elder brother is very sickly, I suppose you would not ask above fifty thousand pounds.'
>
> He answered her in the same style, and the subject dropped.

Although in passages like this – and there are many more of the same kind – Jane Austen condemns the treatment of marriage as a money bargain, she has too clear a knowledge of economic realities to imply that romantic love can safely disregard an income. *Sense and Sensibility* expresses the other side of the picture through Mrs Jennings's comment on the prospect of Edward's continuing in his engagement to Lucy until he gains preferment to a living. Elinor's report of this intention produced from Mrs Jennings the following natural remark.

> 'Wait for his having a living! – aye, we all know how *that* will end; they will wait a twelvemonth, and finding no good comes of it, will set down upon a curacy of fifty pounds a-year, with the interest of his two thousand pounds, and what little matter Mr Steele and Mr Pratt can give her. – Then they will have a child every year! and Lord help 'em! how poor they will be! – I must see what I can give them towards furnishing their

house. Two maids and two men indeed! – as I talked of t'other day. – No, no, they must get a stout girl of all works.'

The problem of deciding how much weight it is reasonable to put on the economic compared with the romantic aspects of marriage is not one to be met by any rule of thumb, and Jane Austen handles the dilemma laughingly in the interchanges between Elizabeth Bennet and her aunt, Mrs Gardiner, when they discuss Wickham's transference of his attentions from Elizabeth to a girl who has unexpectedly inherited £10,000. Previously Mrs Gardiner has warned Elizabeth not to grow attached to Wickham:

'Do not involve yourself or endeavour to involve him in an affection which the want of fortune would make so very imprudent. I have nothing to say against *him*; he is a most interesting young man; and if he had the fortune he ought to have, I should think you could not do better. But as it is – you must not let your fancy run away with you.'

Now, however, hearing of his new attentions, she asks:

'what sort of girl is Miss King? I should be sorry to think our friend mercenary.'
'Pray, my dear aunt, what is the difference in matrimonial affairs, between the mercenary and the prudent motive? Where does discretion end, and avarice begin? Last Christmas you were afraid of his marrying me, because it would be imprudent; and now, because he is trying to get a girl with only ten thousand pounds, you want to find out that he is mercenary.'
'If you will only tell me what sort of girl Miss King is, I shall know what to think.'

'She is a very good kind of girl, I believe. I know no harm of her.'

'But he paid her not the smallest attention, till her grandfather's death made her mistress of this fortune?'

'No – why should he? If it was not allowable for him to gain *my* affections, because I had no money, what occasion could there be for making love to a girl whom he did not care about, and who was equally poor?'

'But there seems indelicacy in directing his attentions towards her, so soon after this event.'

'A man in distressed circumstances has not time for all those elegant decorums which other people may observe. If *she* does not object to it, why should *we*?

'*Her* not objecting does not justify *him*. It only shews her being deficient in something herself – sense or feeling.'

Although the tone of this interchange is bantering, the problem – the insoluble problem – is one that concerns Jane Austen very seriously elsewhere in *Pride and Prejudice*, most notably in the marriage of Charlotte Lucas and Mr Collins. Here the tone could hardly be more serious:

It was a long time before she became at all reconciled to the idea of so unsuitable a match. The strangeness of Mr Collins's making two offers of marriage within three days, was nothing in comparison of his being now accepted. She had always felt that Charlotte's opinion of matrimony was not exactly her own, but she could not have supposed it possible that when called into action, she would have sacrificed every better feeling to worldly advantage. Charlotte the wife of Mr Collins, was a most humiliating picture! – And to the pang of a friend disgracing herself and sunk in her esteem, was added the distressing conviction that it was impossible for that friend to be tolerably happy in the lot she had chosen.

And we are told a few pages later that 'Her disappointment in Charlotte made her turn with fonder regard to her sister, of whose rectitude and delicacy she was sure her opinion could never be shaken.'

Had the episode ended here we should have received a much simpler impression of Jane Austen's attitude than in the end we do. For the visit that Elizabeth pays, at first reluctantly, to Charlotte in her married home shows her gradually coming to see that Charlotte has managed to create at least a tolerable way of life for herself by adroitly minimizing her contacts with Mr Collins and by absorbing herself in household affairs and in the attentions to Lady Catherine that may result in better livings for Mr Collins and greater worldly prosperity.

The Collins's marriage is one of those unromantic, often disillusioned partnerships that Jane Austen presents as a usual feature of social life. Commonly the husband has been trapped into an unrewarding marriage by the superficial attractiveness of his wife as a girl. In *Mansfield Park* Maria Ward who 'had the good luck to captivate Sir Thomas Bertram' has nothing to contribute to his life beyond placid self-centredness and obedience to his instructions as far as she can understand them. In *Sense and Sensibility* Mr Palmer is less fortunate. Elinor, deciding that he is less ill-natured and ill-bred than he pretends to be, reflects:

> His temper might, perhaps, be a little soured by finding, like many others of his sex, that through some unaccountable bias in favour of beauty, he was the husband of a very silly woman; but she knew that this kind of blunder was too common for any sensible man to be lastingly hurt by it.

In *Pride and Prejudice,*

> Had Elizabeth's opinion been all drawn from her own family, she could not have formed a very pleasing picture of conjugal felicity or domestic comfort. Her father, captivated by youth and beauty, and that appearance of good humour, which youth and beauty generally give, had married a woman whose weak understanding and illiberal mind, had very early in their marriage put an end to all real affection for her. Respect, esteem, and confidence, had vanished for ever; and all his views of domestic happiness were overthrown.

The picture is one of great disillusionment, and such marriages *might* break up, as the Rushworths' did, or that of Colonel Brandon's sister-in-law. In general, however, they were expected to be stable, and Mrs Jennings, exposed to Mr Palmer's rudeness, can be explicit about his fate:

> 'Aye, you may abuse me as you please,' said the good-natured old lady, 'you have taken Charlotte off my hands, and cannot give her back again. So there I have the whip hand of you.'
> Charlotte laughed heartily to think that her husband could not get rid of her; and exultingly said, she did not care how cross he was to her, as they must live together.

Despite Jane Austen's disillusioned view of marriage as it commonly presented itself, the dramatic tension of her novels comes from the conflict between the ideal of romantic love and the practice of marrying for social or economic advantage. That conflict was no new thing in English society. The letters of Dorothy Osborne to William Temple give it lasting and magnificent expression. Much earlier in English social history the Pastons were faced with the same conflict in the defiant and ultimately successful determination of Margery Paston to marry Richard Calle in spite of his being 'in trade'.

The romantic attachment of two young people might form the highlight in the contrast between the two conceptions of marriage, but something more lasting and more firmly anchored in realities is implied by Jane Austen as the real alternative to marriage as an economic partnership and family alliance. She hints at it, though lightheartedly, in the affectionate marriages of the Crofts and the Harvilles in *Persuasion*, where the relation between husband and wife remains strongly personal, not a matter of playing the social roles ascribed to husband and wife; and where, because their interpersonal relation has not been dissipated in other social roles, they remain more strongly tied to each other than either is to anyone else. More gravely and movingly she implies her ideal in the deep concern of Mr Bennet when he fears that Elizabeth is accepting Mr Darcy for his rank and wealth:

'let me advise you to think better of it. I know your disposition, Lizzy. I know that you could be neither happy nor respectable, unless you truly esteemed your husband; unless you looked up to him as a superior. Your lively talents would place you in the greatest danger in an unequal marriage. You could scarcely escape discredit and misery. My child, let me not have the grief of seeing *you* unable to respect your partner in life. You know not what you are about.'

The scene parallels Sir Thomas Bertram's similar warning to Maria, an ineffectual warning because of the different personalities and relationships of the two fathers and daughters; and Maria's disgrace is the kind of disaster Mr Bennet fears. But Mr Bennet's speech is interesting for its inconsistency, one of those valuable inconsistencies which may not be noticed by an author but serve to convey something more than the simplest sense he set out to express. Mr Bennet first insists that Elizabeth must be able to esteem her husband, to look up to him as a superior, and this expresses a rather patriarchal concept of marriage, but a moment afterwards he glances at his own unhappy marriage: 'let me not have the grief of seeing *you* unable to respect your partner in life.' He echoes what we have been previously told of his disillusionment with his wife: 'Respect, esteem, and confidence, had vanished for ever; and all his views of domestic happiness were overthrown.' In other words, the ideal conveyed is one of mutual respect, the sort of respect bred in Elizabeth and Darcy by what each has done for the other's education.

It is largely through the family that a society passes on its established values to the child, and some of those are likely to be values that the family itself fulfils only very imperfectly in its own behaviour. The child may learn that lying and malicious gossip are bad but it may also see its parents engaging in them. Most children acquiesce and easily arrive at the sort of compromise they find exemplified in adult behaviour: lip service is paid to the established social standards, whilst actual behaviour falls well below them but without violating them too grossly. Some children, however – perhaps many children in some limited fields of behaviour – remain in a state of conflict between the ideals they have been taught and the behaviour of people they are supposed to respect, perhaps the very people from whom they learnt the ideals, and characteristically their parents. George Fox provides a notable example, in his rigid adherence to principles he had absorbed in childhood but found so little exemplified that he founded a new religious sect to uphold them.

Many sensitive and intelligent children must be in the position of being more sensitive and intelligent than their parents. But probably many more believe they are. It is not uncommon for the child to harbour the conviction that he is so superior to the family in which he has grown up that he cannot really be a child of that family at all. This is a common theme of folk tales, the foundling princess theme, and it represents a fantasy harboured at some time during childhood by very many children. It frequently crops up in literature; *The Winter's Tale* is an instance of the kind of story that encourages the fantasy, and Eliot uses the idea for comic effect in *The Confidential Clerk* when he makes Lady Elizabeth say that she had always felt in some way different from her family and could never believe that she was just the daughter of an ordinary earl.

The basic idea of a child who is wiser or more sensitive and civilized or of finer moral fibre than the parents occurs in several of Jane Austen's novels. In *Northanger Abbey* it is not the heroine but the hero, Henry Tilney, who has finer values than his father and has to defy him. But in the other novels we can see Jane Austen gradually exploring (with, in the end greatly increased realism and freedom from fantasy) the problem of the relation of the daughter to a mother who is less able or less sensitive than herself. In the earlier novels she simplifies the problem by heavily emphasizing the deficiencies of the mother figure. Mrs Dashwood, though genuinely affectionate, is almost as romantically ill-judging as the 16-year-old Marianne; Mrs Bennet is a woman 'of mean understanding, little information, and uncertain temper'; Fanny Price's mother and aunts are all in different ways contemptible. In *Emma*, however, a change begins. Though motherless, the heroine has had in Mrs Weston a mother-figure to whom she avowedly owes a great deal ('Astonished that the person who had brought me up should be a gentlewoman!') even though she has never felt the obligation to be guided by her as fully as she would have done with a real mother (Mr Knightley remarks that she always had her own way).

The relation, however, has become one of equal friendship by the time the story begins, not a parental relation.
And, despite the heroine's superiority to her father, a
contrasting note comes in with Emma's deluded conviction that Harriet Smith must be of gentle birth; it is the
heroine who becomes a little ridiculous through believing
too readily that she has discovered a foundling princess.
Persuasion is still more interesting from this point of view.
Although very obviously a finer person than her father
and sisters, Anne Elliot is given, in Lady Russell, a mother
figure whom she has grown up greatly respecting and
loving with spontaneous affection; a mother figure, moreover, who appreciates her quality and sees her superiority
to the rest of the family. Jane Austen here provides her
heroine with as adequate a mother-figure as a girl could
reasonably expect, though of course one with limitations;
and it is within this framework that she examines the
problem of the child who receives guidance from a parent
less sensitively wise than herself. Of all the novels it forms
the most mature and considered examination of the
problem. The duty of obedience is not questioned; Anne
is made to tell Captain Wentworth that she cannot
reproach herself for having taken her godmother's advice.
She is too respectful and too fairminded to say outright
that the advice was wrong; it was the kind of situation in
which advice is right or wrong according as events turn
out. But – without complete consistency – she goes on to
say that she herself would never give such advice, so
certain of immediate evil and uncertain of future good. In
saying this she does in fact plainly imply that she has
standards of judgment which Lady Russell cannot share
and by which her crucial advice stands condemned. It
amounts to a decisive statement that even a child whose
mother by ordinary standards seems sensible and good
must, if she is of the quality of heroines, ignore parental
advice and follow her own lights.

However, the maturity of *Persuasion* is evident in the fact that the heroine has herself contributed to the sorrow of the broken engagement and the estrangement. She has her share in the responsibility: she has yielded to persuasion. This is Captain Wentworth's reproach. And, in spite of Anne's claim that she was right to have yielded, the whole tenor of the novel suggests that there was a problem here, that she had no clear-cut obligation to accept her godmother's advice. The traditional tension between romantic love and marriage guided by the family has always assumed the possibility of justified resistance to family and parental pressures, and this is implicit throughout *Persuasion*.

The problem is faced more squarely in that novel than it is in *Mansfield Park* where it appears in a rather different form. Fanny Price is under great pressure not only from the less worthy members of the family but from those she most loves and respects, Sir Thomas and Edmund, to accept Henry Crawford's offer of marriage. Against their persuasion she can oppose only her secret love of Edmund himself and her distrust of the worldliness of the Crawfords. We are given to understand that Henry might in the end have succeeded, that Fanny would have sacrificed her apparently hopeless love and have yielded to the family's persuasion had not Crawford's worldliness trapped him into the affair with Maria and exposed him beyond any condonation. The crucial problem of the conflict between Fanny's love and her wish to be guided by her family is evaded by this partly accidental exposure of Henry Crawford. In fact we are told of Henry that:

> Could he have found sufficient exultation in overcoming the reluctance, in working himself into the esteem and tenderness of Fanny Price, there would have been every probability of success and felicity for him ... Would he have persevered, and uprightly,

Fanny must have been his reward – and a reward very voluntarily bestowed – within a reasonable period from Edmund's marrying Mary.

Had this in fact been the ending it would have run counter to the values we have been invited to share all through the earlier part of the novel.

Anne Elliot is a much more complex and interesting heroine than Fanny Price because she has in fact done what Fanny was tempted to do – yielded to parental persuasion against the claim of romantic love. It is from that point that *Persuasion* begins. And whereas Fanny is a too perfect heroine, saved more or less by chance at two crucial points from making a mistake, Anne is shown to have made the mistake and to be herself responsible for the unhappiness resulting from the failure to be loyal to her own convinced love. She has therefore a gravity and a sadness that distinguish her from the rather conventionally oppressed, rather prim and self-righteous Fanny who has nothing to reproach herself with and nothing to endure but untoward circumstances and oppression by unworthy people.

The fantasy of the foundling princess implies criticism of the parents and expresses the child's difficulty in reconciling his longing for perfect adorable parents with his experience of hostility towards those he has and his possibly quite rational criticism of much about them. This ambivalence of the parents, especially the mother, is dealt with in fairy tales by the expedient of splitting the mother-figure, as in the story of Cinderella, endowing a dead mother with all the loveable attributes and a wicked stepmother with all the hateful qualities. The father is treated as well meaning but weak or deceived. I once suggested that the Cinderella theme, which has close psychological relations with the foundling princess theme, was equally important in Jane Austen's writings. But I now think I was wrong. It is true that *Mansfield Park* contains many elements of the Cinderella story – with Mrs Norris as the wicked stepmother, an oppressed heroine, and Maria and Julia in the position of the two ugly sisters – but it contains no suggestion of a worthy mother. Splitting the ambivalent mother was not Jane Austen's method. More commonly the heroine is self-created and owes little to maternal training and example – Elinor Dashwood, Elizabeth Bennet, Fanny Price, Emma, Anne Elliot, are either motherless or have had to acquire standards other than those their mothers could have inculcated. This self-created quality in the heroine is characteristic of the foundling princess rather than Cinderella. In working through the problem of a girl whose standards are for some reason higher than those of her parents, Jane Austen dealt with a central tension in the family situation of gifted children. It formed a central point of concentric circles of family life: the close physical proximity and lack of privacy, the authority of the parents, the influence of an extended family, and the implications of all this for marriage based on romantic love.

CHAPTER 3

The Social Habitat in Jane Austen: Distant and Nearer Contexts

After moments of high intensity in her novels Jane Austen commonly allows the heroine a period, often half an hour, of quiet reflection in which to give the events their proper place in her order of values and recover her emotional balance; and she then returns to the social world where abstraction, self-absorption and extremes of feeling are not in place. The immediate social world presses close. The foreground of the novels is thickly peopled and many of the devices for conveying action and character are adapted to that condition and depend upon it. The drawing rooms, for instance, become something like an eighteenth century stage where separate groups and pairs can converse apart, overheard if necessary or in safe privacy if the action demands that. Elinor can contrive her private talk with Lucy Steele under cover of Marianne's piano playing while the others in Lady Middleton's party are at cards. Mrs Musgrove, in their sitting room at the White Hart, 'was giving Mrs Croft the history of her eldest daughter's engagement, and just in that inconvenient tone of voice which was perfectly audible while it pretended to be a whisper', and both Anne and Captain Wentworth had their attention caught when the two middle-aged ladies agreed in condemning a long engagement. And then the quiet conversation between Anne and Captain Harville is overheard by Captain Wentworth, with decisive results.

Social adroitness for avoiding involvement in a conversation were necessary too. Jane Fairfax keeps in the background while Frank Churchill flounders around his blunder about Mr Perry's carriage, and Mr Knightley with his suspicion aroused glances back at her: 'From Frank Churchill's face, where he thought he saw confusion suppressed or laughed away, he had involuntarily turned to hers; but she was indeed behind, and too busy with her shawl.' After the secret engagement is acknowledged Frank Churchill teases Jane by reminding Emma of his blunder:

> and it was evident from Jane's countenance that she too was really hearing him, though trying to seem deaf.
> 'Such an extraordinary dream of mine?' he cried, 'I can never think of it without laughing. – She hears us, Miss Woodhouse. I see it in her cheek, her smile, her vain attempt to frown.'

It is Jane's engagement, again, that allows Mrs Elton to take the supposedly private conversation in a drawing room to its ridiculous extreme in her pretence at private communication with Jane and her aunt, excluding Emma, in the Bates's crowded little living room.

In part these devices in their great variety represent the eighteenth century stage transposed to the novel, in part no doubt they are based on the real conditions and conventions of the time. They arise out of the densely social foreground of the novels. This, with the immediate family at its nucleus, rewards close examination, but its main features are clear and my intention here is to take it for granted and give more attention to the distance and the middle distance of the social scene.

The standard Victorian account of Jane Austen implied almost that there was no social distance, no sense in her novels of a wider social setting than the few families in a country neighbourhood that she preferred to work with; and it would pose a critical problem if we found that her people really were isolated in their small concerns and insulated from things around them in a way that made their world unreal or artificial, an encapsulated never-never village. We should then have to ask very seriously, as we may have to in much of Henry James, what is gained and what is lost by the limitation. But in reality her villages and the neighbourhoods of which they form part never are isolated. Their contacts with the outer world, especially the more sophisticated world of London and the watering places, always form a vital part of the plot and machinery of the novels and still more of their moral themes, especially through the contrast between smart, worldly values and the appeal of quiet friendships and the stability of settled families. For her the small neighbourhood is not a vignette with the background faded out, but a focus, or a nodal point from which lines radiate into the wider society.

The more distant features of the scene, the larger national events and the social movements of the period, are certainly not her central interest – she was not a political journalist – but they count for her in so far as they are naturally assimilated into the lives of the people she lived among and fashioned into fictional characters. Mrs John Dashwood, wanting to bestow a mark of favour, but of course economically, on Lucy Steele and her sister 'had given each of them a needle book, made by some emigrant' – and we glimpse for a moment the plight of the French emigrés dependent on the charity of a Mrs John Dashwood. The British slave trade had been abolished, after fierce contention, some six years before *Emma* was written. Not being Harriet Beecher Stowe, Jane Austen was not directly concerned with the problem, but she presents quite naturally and effortlessly the general revulsion of feeling against slavery and the careful trimming of their sails to this new wind by people whose money, coming from Bristol, might be suspect. Mrs

Elton's sensitiveness on the subject makes her see a reference where none was meant: 'Oh! my dear, human flesh! You quite shock me; if you mean a fling at the slave-trade, I assure you Mr Suckling was always rather a friend to the abolition.' The Napoleonic Wars come in with the presence of militia regiments and their effects on the local girls and again with the peace of 1814 'turning all our rich Navy Officers ashore'. Duelling was an obsolescent but still living institution, and when Colonel Brandon challenges Willoughby we might, from a simpler novelist, have had a dramatic account of the seconds, the secrecy, the shots that missed, and this, I suppose, would have shown that Jane Austen was really in touch with the world. What we get is a most illuminating, though apparently undeliberated, picture of civilized social opinion balanced uneasily around a controversial institution. Elinor asks Colonel Brandon whether he has seen Mr Willoughby since they were at Barton:

> 'Yes,' he replied gravely, 'once I have. One meeting was unavoidable.' Elinor, startled by his manner, looked at him anxiously, saying, 'What? have you met him to – '
> 'I could meet him in no other way. Eliza had confessed to me, though most reluctantly, the name of her lover; and when he returned to town, which was within a fortnight after myself, we met by appointment, he to defend, I to punish his conduct. We returned unwounded, and the meeting, therefore, never got abroad.'
> Elinor sighed over the fancied necessity of this; but to a man and a soldier, she presumed not to censure it.

The brief exchange puts the broad institution and the flux of opinion about it into the perspective of ordinary civilized lives at a particular period of time. The great events enter her novels through their effects on people who had their personal lives to live – rather than performing like journalists' puppets on the stage of history in the making.

The Austen family were not in the least out of touch with public events. They were closely connected with Warren Hastings; the husband of Jane Austen's cousin died by the guillotine during the Terror; one of her brothers was a militia officer and two others were naval officers on active service against the French. Her attitude to such things as material for her novels is clear enough when, in writing to Cassandra about *Pride and Prejudice*, she suggests that it would have been better with some contrasting shade here and there 'with a long chapter of sense, if it could be had; if not, of solemn specious nonsense, about something unconnected with the story; an essay on writing, a critique on Walter Scott, or the history of Buonaparté.' (4 February 1813). The people who feel that her work would have been in some way more significant if she had dealt directly with contemporary great events are coming perilously close to the Prince Regent's Librarian with his suggestion that she should write an 'historical romance, illustrative of the history of the august House of Coburg' (27 March 1816). The affairs of the nation which General Tilney says he may be poring over for hours after Catherine is asleep are not the material of her fiction, but when they affect the lives of her characters she easily encompasses them in her view. This is perhaps what John Bayley implies when he says (Southam, ed., *Critical Essays on Jane Austen*, 1968) that her world has the 'power of effortless expansion, the negligent authority of a world that is possessed without being contemplated'.

Between the distant events of national importance and the immediate context of the heroine's family and close associates there lies a middle distance of social life which forms an important part of the setting of several of the novels and raises issues to which present day readers are likely to be sensitive. In particular, in this middle distance, questions arise about social class and the relations of people to each other within a system where rank was an important part of the individual's identity; until his position in society was known he was incompletely, very incompletely, defined. The question of Jane Austen's attitude to the relative importance of a person's social class and his other attributes affects our enjoyment and critical assessment of her work because she is modern enough to be challenged by our own values and relevant to our own problems about social class. Is she, for instance, a snob, in the sense of contentedly seeing people judged, and their opportunities defined, by their social position rather than their individual qualities? She is near enough to us not to be exempt from this kind of question, which would hardly arise with, say, Shakespeare.

Ultimately social rank needed economic backing. Although prosperity was not enough to secure acceptance into the gentry it took a tradesman a long way in that direction. The unreality of the scruples that some gentlemen might feel is satirized in Mr John Dashwood's dealings with Mrs Jennings, whose real vulgarities he couldn't discern:

> She seems a most valuable woman indeed. – Her house, her style of living, all bespeak an exceeding good income.

When he also met her daughter, Lady Middleton, who concentrates anxiously on every elegance that may distinguish her from her mother, Mr John Dashwood's doubts are finally swept away and he concludes that although Mrs Jennings is not so elegant as her daughter she is 'an exceeding well-behaved woman' and he decides that his wife:

> need not have any scruple even of visiting *her*, which, to say the truth, has been a little the case, and very naturally; for we only knew that Mrs Jennings was the widow of a man who had got all his money in a low way.

Here the conflict around prosperity gained from trade is material for simple satire. At another point Jane Austen shows approval of Mrs Jennings's loyalty to the friends she had when the family was in trade: 'excepting a few old city friends, whom, to Lady Middleton's regret, she had never dropped, she visited no one, to whom an introduction could at all discompose the feelings of her two young companions.'

It was, very evidently, a period of change in the relative weight to be allowed to birth and to personal qualities, with consequent uncertainties which Jane Austen reflects and at times seems perhaps to share. In *Persuasion* Sir Walter's snobbery and Mary's pathetic clinging to her precedence among the Musgroves are condemned without hesitation because they overstress the importance of birth among people whose standards of behaviour and education put them within the same broad category of the gentry. Nor can she give much weight even to noble birth unaccompanied by more personal distinctions. When Sir Walter and Elizabeth gloatingly display their re-established contact with the Dalrymples:

> Anne was ashamed. Had Lady Dalrymple and her daughter even been very agreeable, she would still have been ashamed of the agitation they created, but they were nothing. There was no superiority of manner,

accomplishment, or understanding. Lady Dalrymple had acquired the name of 'a charming woman', because she had a smile and civil answer for every body. Miss Carteret, with still less to say, was so plain and so awkward, that she would never have been tolerated in Camden-place but for her birth.

Anne's standards are then worked out by the contrast with Lady Russell's and still more Mr Elliot's:

> 'My idea of good company, Mr Elliot, is the company of clever, well-informed people, who have a great deal of conversation: that is what I call good company.'
>
> 'You are mistaken,' said he gently, 'that is not good company, that is the best. Good company requires only birth, education and manners, and with regard to education is not very nice. Birth and good manners are essential; but a little learning is by no means a dangerous thing in good company, on the contrary, it will do very well. My cousin, Anne, shakes her head. She is not satisfied. She is fastidious.'

All this is straightforward, easily acceptable by modern standards. But another passage in the same novel shows a difference. Mrs Smith is describing Mr Elliot's first marriage, which is purely for the sake of the money his wife would bring him. Anne interrupts to ask:

> 'But was not she a very low woman?'
>
> 'Yes; which I objected to, but he would not regard. Money, money, was all that he wanted. Her father was a grazier, her grandfather had been a butcher, but that was all nothing. She was a fine woman, had had a decent education, was brought forward by some cousins, thrown by chance into Mr Elliot's company, and fell in love with him; and not a difficulty or a

scruple was there on his side, with respect to her birth. All his caution was spent in being secured of the real amount of her fortune, before he committed himself.'

Mrs Smith and Anne Elliot undoubtedly share the feeling that Mr Elliot degraded himself by the marriage, and we are meant to accept that view. It is a case, however, where money alone, without mutual love, is set in the scales against birth, and for money alone Mr Elliot willingly disregarded a social position – his being heir to a baronetcy – which Jane Austen thought a man should value. Mrs Smith goes on:

'Depend upon it, whatever esteem Mr Elliot may have for his own situation in life now, as a young man he had not the smallest value for it. His chance of the Kellynch estate was something, but all the honour of the family he held as cheap as dirt. I have often heard him declare, that if baronetcies were saleable, any body should have his for fifty pounds, arms and motto, name and livery included.'

She sees it as a privilege which, conferred by birth and not to be earned, must yet be deserved if the recipient of the privilege is to be respected in his own person. She shows that Mr Elliot is unworthy of the privilege, and this is exactly the attitude she expresses towards Sir Walter Elliot when in the end she sums him up as 'a foolish, spendthrift baronet, who had not had principle or sense enough to maintain himself in the situation in which Providence had placed him'.

When social rank is set against mutual love, of course she takes a different view. Much of the dramatic tension of the novels comes from the conflict between the ideal of romantic love and the practice of marrying for social or economic advantage. That conflict was a real enough thing in English social history; Dorothy Osborne's letters give it lasting and magnificent expression, and the Pastons much earlier were faced with the same problem in the defiant and ultimately successful determination of Margery Paston to marry Richard Calle in spite of his being 'in trade'.

Jane Austen is on the side of romantic love. But she never ignores economic realities and never romanticizes married poverty – Mrs Jennings's forecast of the fate of Edward Ferrars and Lucy Steele if they marry on his small living makes that clear. Nor, perhaps to our discomfort, does she dismiss social class and standing as unimportant between lovers. Consider Elizabeth Bennet with Lady Catherine in the shrubbery. 'If you were sensible of your own good,' says Lady Catherine, denouncing Elizabeth's supposed determination to marry Mr Darcy, 'you would not wish to quit the sphere, in which you have been brought up.' An angry and contemptuous girl of our own time, exposed to similar rudeness and snobbery, would be likely to denounce the ridiculous irrelevance to herself and her lover of any such consideration. Elizabeth on the contrary takes the problem seriously and argues her case: 'In marrying your nephew, I should not consider myself as quitting that sphere. He is a gentleman; I am a gentleman's daughter; so far we are equal.' Lady Catherine has to accept that and argue her own case more thoroughly. A family in that sphere might have the asset of marriage connections with the nobility – Lady Catherine herself was of noble birth – or the liability of connections with people in trade. So Lady Catherine replies 'True. You *are* a gentleman's daughter. But who was your mother? Who are your uncles and aunts? Do not imagine me ignorant of their condition.' One of her uncles was Mr Gardiner, 'a man who lived by trade, and within view of his own warehouses'. And it became part of Mr Darcy's education to discover how completely acceptable he was by the standards of gentlemen.

It is in *Emma* that social distinctions and the problems connected with them are most evidently not incidental but part of the tissue of the story as they were part of the tissue of the social life that gave Jane Austen her materials. The Woodhouses and Mr Knightley set the standard; they provide the anchoring point for all the social comparisons. There are greater families in the outer orbit of the story, the Churchills and those they associate with, but they exist as hearsay; and there is the more sophisticated world of London and fashionable watering places, but it too is peripheral. For the neighbourhood of Highbury, and for Jane Austen, Hartfield and Donwell Abbey are the criterion of good breeding without smart sophistication, of the good social behaviour that includes good moral principles, and of good manners based on a genuine consideration for others. It is from this standard that Emma lapses so badly in the Box Hill party. Mr Woodhouse is benevolent without condescension. He is glad of the Bates's and Mrs Goddard for his gossip and quadrille; Mrs Goddard, the mistress of a school, had 'formerly owed much to Mr Woodhouse's kindness', and about the Bates's Mr Woodhouse says regretfully 'It is a great pity that their circumstances should be so confined! a great pity indeed! and I have often wished – but it is so little one can venture to do – small, trifling presents, of any thing uncommon' and he goes on to discuss the Hartfield pork he is sending them. Emma's good feelings are rather more tinged with condescension; her 'bestowing' a quarter of an hour's call on an old servant, her charitable visit to the sick family with Harriet, even her search of the Hartfield stores for something that might tempt Jane Fairfax to eat, these have a touch of the Lady Bountiful; but although the manner is more dominating than her father's there is no suggestion of any lapse from real kindness of intention. These incidences are part of the good social behaviour in which she has been trained, not part of the intolerable snobbery which she has to outgrow in the course of the novel.

The social gradations which are so prominent in the background and sometimes in the foreground of the story are in the main registered through Emma's eyes. This creates a special twist for the reader since many of her judgments are laudable and obviously offered as congenial (she is, after all, the heroine) – while others reflect the over-confidence and self-satisfaction which contribute to her blunders and her lapses, and the correction of which comes about with the personality development that forms the substance of the novel. *Emma*, consequently, is the kind of novel in which it may be difficult to gain a just impression of the values that the author offers for approval. When Emma decides after two meetings that Mrs Elton is vain, 'that she meant to shine and be very superior, but with manners which had been formed in a bad school, pert and familiar', we are obviously meant to agree; when she disparages Robert Martin to Harriet we are meant to see that she is being snobbish; but there's more uncertainty when she assures Frank Churchill that there isn't enough good society in the neighbourhood to make balls at the Crown possible,

'and even when particulars were given and families described, he was still unwilling to admit that the inconvenience of such a mixture would be any thing, or that there would be the smallest difficulty in every body's returning into their proper place the next morning ... He seemed to have all the life and spirit, cheerful feelings, and social inclinations of his father, and nothing of the pride or reserve of Enscombe. Of pride, indeed, there was, perhaps, scarcely enough; his indifference to a confusion of rank, bordered too much on inelegance of mind. He could be no judge, however, of the evil he was holding cheap. It was but an effusion of lively spirits.'

The passage is complicated by the fact that Frank Churchill's apparent disregard for social distinctions arises simply from his determination to arrange a ball where he can have some time in Jane Fairfax's company; we are not being invited to disapprove of Emma's insistence on maintaining the decorum of social distinctions. And yet the tone is ambiguous; 'the evil he was holding cheap' may be meant to sound excessive. On the other hand, to say that Frank Churchill could be no judge of the evil he was holding cheap may only draw attention to the ease with which the more exalted families like his could maintain their social position, however much they chose to unbend, whereas in a village neighbourhood the better families – better by the standards of social intercourse that manners, education and leisure made possible – had to be much more guarded and watchful if, in trade union terms, the socially skilled were not to suffer dilution.

The ambiguity in this passage is by no means of the kind we know too well in some novelists where moral shuffling and 'lightness of touch' allow the middlebrow reader to feel undisturbed while the sophisticated can enjoy a superior disregard of moral standards. That way aestheticism lies, and it had no appeal for Jane Austen. If there are ambiguities in *Emma* they arise from the complexity of the social materials as she viewed them.

A vital aspect of Emma's growing up undoubtedly consists in her learning to be less of a snob. Yet the seriousness with which we are invited to take social distinctions is evident, after the dénouement, in the comments on Harriet's parentage. Emma's early over-valuation of the girl was accompanied by the conviction that she must be the natural daughter of a gentleman. The disclosure, upon her engagement to Robert Martin, of her actual parentage is made to emphasize Emma's complete misjudgment and provide a further reason for her contrition:

> She proved to be the daughter of a tradesman, rich enough to afford her the comfortable maintenance which had ever been hers, and decent enough to have always wished for concealment. – Such was the blood of gentility which Emma had formerly been so ready to vouch for! – It was likely to be as untainted perhaps as the blood of many a gentleman: but what a connexion had she been preparing for Mr Knightley – or for the Churchills – or even for Mr Elton! – The stain of illegitimacy, unbleached by nobility or wealth, would have been a stain indeed.

Mr Knightley distinguishes between Emma's vain spirit (which she has accused herself of having) and her serious spirit: 'Not your vain spirit, but your serious spirit. – If one leads you wrong, I am sure the other tells you of it.' Clearly we are meant to assume that it is her serious spirit which recognizes the shame it would have meant even for Mr Elton to marry not an illegitimate girl – Emma had knowingly planned that for him – but the illegitimate daughter of a tradesman. And yet there is a difficulty here, because Mr Knightley, the novel's paragon of sound judgment, who had no illusions about Harriet's birth (and felt it a disadvantage even for Robert Martin), had been able to tell Emma that in choosing Harriet for Mr Elton she would have done better for him than he did for himself in marrying his Augusta.

I doubt whether a clash like this has to be resolved. Jane Austen was not working out a consistent system; Emma's contrition for her deluded conviction about Harriet is natural where it occurs, and so too, in its context, is Mr

Knightley's judgment that Harriet is a far worthier person than Mrs Elton. But Emma's feeling that Harriet as a tradesman's illegitimate daughter will do very well for Mr Martin but would have been a come-down for Mr Elton does mean that Jane Austen considers it reasonable to attach serious importance to gradations of social standing in her world even when the personal worth of her characters bore no correspondence to their relative rank.

It was a socially hierarchical world. But, as this novel in particular demonstrates, the hierarchy was not fixed; people and families could rise and sink, and the boundary between gentry and people in trade could be crossed. The social fluidity is emphasized in *Emma* by the large number of characters, important and less important, whose transitional or marginal position in the social hierarchy Jane Austen draws to our attention. There are the flagrantly *nouveaux riches* of Maple Grove, themselves of course incensed against their neighbourhood's upstarts who have, says Mrs Elton, only just arrived, 'and yet by their manners they evidently think themselves equal even to my brother, Mr Suckling, who happens to be one of their nearest neighbours. It is infinitely too bad. Mr Suckling, who has been 11 years a resident at Maple Grove, and whose father had it before him – I believe, at least – I am almost sure that old Mr Suckling had completed the purchase before his death.' Mr Elton too was on his way up. Reflecting on her blunder is not realizing it was she he wanted to marry, Emma admits that she had often thought 'his manners to herself unnecessarily gallant; but it had passed as his way, as a mere error of judgment, of knowledge, of taste, as one proof among many others that he had not always lived in the best society, that with all the gentleness of his address, true elegance was sometimes wanting' Among the minor characters Mr Perry, the apothecary, is at least rising in prosperity. When Frank Churchill lets slip an item from Jane Fairfax's clandestine correspondence, Mr Weston breaks in: '"What is this?" cried Mr Weston, "about Perry and a carriage? Is Perry going to set up his carriage, Frank? I am glad he can afford it."'. Mr Weston's own history is detailed at the beginning of the novel in terms less of the personal relation his first marriage brought than of the fact that although seeming 'an amazing match' in connecting him with the Churchills, it proved too expensive to him and led him to quit the militia and engage in trade. Only after 20 years he had made enough money to live like a gentleman again; his fluctuations of status and the fact that his second wife has been a governess (and is also Emma's closest friend), present an example early in the novel of this crossing and blurring of social boundaries which repeatedly recurs.

One of its recurrences, merging with an early check to Emma's snobbishness, provides an almost explicit statement of the importance of the facts of social standing and the pressures which led the established families to acquiesce in changes, changes based fundamentally on money but not easily secured by money alone:

> This was the occurrence: – The Coles had been settled some years in Highbury, and were very good sort of people – friendly, liberal, and unpretending; but, on the other hand, they were of low origin, in trade, and only moderately genteel. On their first coming into the country, they had lived in proportion to their income, quietly, keeping little company and that little unexpensively; but the last year or two had brought them a considerable increase of means – the house in town had yielded greater profits, and fortune in general had smiled on them. With their wealth, their views increased; their want of a larger house, their inclination for more company. They added to their house, to their number of servants, to their expenses of every sort; and by this time were, in fortune and style of living, second

only to the family at Hartfield. Their love of society, and their new dining-room, prepared every body for their keeping dinner-company; and a few parties, chiefly among the single men, had already taken place. The regular and best families Emma could hardly suppose they would presume to invite – neither Donwell, nor Hartfield, nor Randalls. Nothing should tempt *her* to go, even if they did; and she regretted that her father's known habits would be giving her refusal less meaning than she could wish. The Coles were very respectable in their way, but they ought to be taught that it was not for them to arrange the terms on which the superior families would visit them. This lesson, she very much feared, they would receive only from herself; she had little hope of Mr Knightley, none of Mr Weston.

The wind is taken out of her sails when all the other families are asked to dinner and she and her father receive no invitation. 'She felt that she should like to have had the power of refusal; and afterwards, as the idea of the party to be assembled there, consisting precisely of those whose society was dearest to her, occurred again and again, she did not know that she might not have been tempted to accept'. When at last the invitation does arrive, very deferentially phrased, she is only too glad to be persuaded by her friends to accept. The dinner of course serves the development of Jane Austen's plot, but the little episode is also a summary statement of Highbury's social mobility: with Emma's acceptance the Coles have arrived.

Downward shifts on the social scale were equally possible, as Jane Austen herself knew too well, having undergone the change from being the daughter of a well-to-do rector to being, with her mother and sister, poor relations dependent on her wealthy brother for a small cottage near his estate, and only too glad of it after some years of lodgings and shared houses. Miss Bates, Mr Knightley reminds Emma, 'is poor: she has sunk from the comforts she was born to; and, if she live to old age, must probably sink more'. Jane Fairfax too is in a precarious social position, a poor orphan, brought up as a gentle-woman but not fancying the prospect of being a governess, descending into a dreadful non-world between the family and the servants. The settling of *her* social status is one of the main threads in the novel, and it is a pivotal comic point when Emma says to Frank Churchill, 'You know Miss Fairfax's situation in life, I conclude: what she is destined to be', and he replies 'Yes – (rather hesitatingly) – I believe I do', where Emma foresees her being a governess and he is hoping she will become the future mistress of Enscombe.

No one would want to suggest that *Emma* is 'a novel of social mobility'. *Not* to be preoccupied with abstract social questions is almost a necessary condition of writing a good novel. Equally, not to be aware of social conditions would be disabling – aware of them not just as a background but as part of the habitat whose demands, limiting effects and opportunities to a great extent shape the characters' lives. Jane Austen writes her novels out of the real social situation of her time. Her acceptance of these realities as her inescapable conditions, even when they set up conflicts of feeling and uncertainties of judgment, is part of her excellence. It appears unmistakably in the story of Harriet Smith and Robert Martin and their relations to the other characters. She leaves us in no doubt about the individual superiority of Robert Martin to Mr Elton; Mr Elton's mean behaviour in trying to humiliate Harriet at the ball is contrasted with Robert Martin's delicacy and consideration when he accidentally meets Harriet sheltering in Ford's during a shower, and Mr Elton's letter to Mr Woodhouse after Emma had rejected his proposal, its 'ill-judged solemnity of leave-taking' and the resentment plainly spoken in excluding her from his compliments, contrasts with Robert Martin's letter of proposal to Harriet, the style of which was much above Emma's expectation: 'There were not merely no grammatical errors, but as a composition it would not have disgraced a gentleman; the language, though plain, was strong and unaffected, and the sentiments it conveyed very much to the credit of the writer. It was short, but expressed good sense, warm attachment, liberality, propriety, even delicacy of feeling'. But in the conclusion the Martins are left in a social position which distances them from Emma and her milieu: 'Harriet, necessarily drawn away by her engagements with the Martins, was less and less at Hartfield; which was not to be regretted. – The intimacy between her and Emma must sink; their friendship must change into a calmer sort of goodwill; and, fortunately, what ought to be, and must be, seemed already beginning, and in the most gradual, natural manner.' There can be no doubt that Jane Austen offers this as the right attitude. Robert Martin's range of conversation and information, his reading habits, the quality of his voice and his outward manners would have placed restrictions on the ordinary social interchanges at Hartfield and Randalls.

At the same time Jane Austen shows us how much, without a trace of condescension, Mr Knightley values him. 'He knows I have a thorough regard for him and all his family, and I believe, considers me as one of his best friends . . . I never hear better sense from any one than Robert Martin'. And when ordinary functional contacts make informal social intercourse natural there need be no artificial class barriers – . Mr Knightley tells Emma of Robert Martin's renewed meeting with Harriet:

> 'It is a very simple story. He went to town on business three days ago, and I got him to take charge of some papers which I was wanting to send to John. –

He delivered these papers to John, at his chambers, and was asked by him to join their party the same evening to Astley's. They were going to take the two eldest boys to Astley's. The party was to be our brother and sister, Henry, John – and Miss Smith. My friend Robert could not resist. They called for him on their way; were all extremely amused; and my brother asked him to dine with them the next day – which he did – and in the course of that visit (as I understand) he found an opportunity of speaking to Harriet; and certainly did not speak in vain.'

To mature, well-judging men like the two Knightleys Robert Martin's social standing presented no problem: they would not expect to meet him paying a social call at Hartfield or Randalls but there could be no difficulty about having him to a family dinner when some occasion naturally suggested it. Mr Knightley is far from disregarding Robert Martin's social status and role as a tenant farmer of his. In the same scene with Emma he supposes her still to be disapproving of the match for Harriet and he goes on:

'I am afraid it gives you more pain than you expected. His situation is an evil – but you must consider it as what satisfies your friend; and I will answer for your thinking better and better of him as you know him more. His good sense and good principles would delight you. – As far as the man is concerned, you could not wish your friend in better hands. His rank in society I would alter if I could; which is saying a great deal I assure you, Emma. – You laugh at me about William Larkins; but I could quite as ill spare Robert Martin.'

The society in which *Emma* is set, therefore, is one in which sensible people accept the fact of differences of rank although they recognize personal merit that cuts across those divisions. Moreover, it is a society in which changes of status are going on continuously although gradually, and a man like Mr Knightley accepts the changes as they occur without wanting to hurry them or take short cuts. The Martins, the Coles, Mr Perry, are all moving up the social scale, and Mr Knightley will welcome them at whatever point they may have reached – but he will not seek a short cut to social promotion for them such as Emma attempted with Harriet.

Besides its other extraordinary merits *Emma* has the special interest of going further than the other novels in observing the problems of rank in the society of its time. To be scathing about Lady Catherine or Sir Walter Elliot presented no problems of attitude to a clergyman's daughter. In *Emma* she looked at people below her in the social hierarchy and handled the much more confused and conflict-arousing social distinctions associated with differences of manners, education and range of interest. She makes no attempt at an abstract solution of the conflicts; she simply has her characters working out their personal problems in a context where distinctions of rank and changes of rank were part of the structure and living process of society.

CHAPTER 4

Jane Austen and Moral Judgment

In the period around 1800 the range of permissible values in English culture included the two extremes; exponents of either might deride or abhor the other, but each had its place in the culture of the time and, though attacked, could not be ignored. One of the chief tensions was between conflicting attitudes to emotion and the expression of sentiment. The one valued calm and the seeming security achieved by checking and regulating emotional expression, the other valued the heightened sense of living brought about by a free and even exaggerated expression of emotion.

Behind, and much more important than, the public polemics, lay the private tension felt by cultivated people between the two contrasting outlooks on emotion. It is given admirable expression by Jane Austen (1775–1817) in *Sense and Sensibility*, where the two devoted sisters represent contrasting points of view. Jane Austen (who admired Crabbe to the point of saying that she would have been willing to marry him) undoubtedly comes down in favour of Apollonian sense, but she is able to see its limitations and to show sympathy and understanding for some part of the 'sensibility' of Marianne; it seems likely, of course, that the sisters represented contrasting aspects of herself and probably of other people of her time. She can ridicule the excesses of sensibility without doubting the genuineness of the personality traits that lead to it and without losing sympathy with the person whose emotional life is organized in this way. It is perhaps in the complex attitudes of Jane Austen, whose control may tempt us to overlook her intense vitality, that the subtly extended outlook of finer minds in her culture can best be seen.

It is characteristic of her work that its extraordinarily amusing, entertaining quality is fused intimately with moral seriousness (which rarely lapses into moralizing), and that she has the manner of assuming the same seriousness in her readers. It has, strangely, been possible for readers and critics in the past to overlook this quality, and to discuss her work as if it offered no more than delicately entertaining studies of the surface of polite society and its trivial doings amidst the costumes and architecture of advertisers' Regency. One of the more fatuous of several standard misunderstandings is the complaint that she shows no interest in the great social events of the time – by which is meant the Napoleonic Wars. Apart from the doubt whether these national cataclysms are the important social events, the suggestion itself is inaccurate, for Jane Austen's work in fact gives a convincing impression of the impact of public events on the ordinary lives of middle-class people of the time. There are the militia and the camps, with their effects on the local girls, in *Pride and Prejudice*; the regular Army as a career in *Pride and Prejudice* and *Emma*; still more the Navy as a career, in *Mansfield Park* and *Persuasion*, with the use of influential acquaintance to get the midshipman promoted, young men making their fortunes from prizes, 'this peace' turning them ashore, the hope of another war to bring further promotion and prize-money, their disablement from wounds, the life of their wives and families waiting for them or accompanying them, and the jealousy of established families at the sudden social ascent of successful officers. Nor are the Wars the only great social events to be reflected in their natural contemporary light. The importance of West Indian estates to English incomes has its ordinary unemphasized place, in *Mansfield Park* and

Persuasion, together with the hazards of the journey when the Antigua estate has to be visited. The abolition of slavery echoes in a form that reveals exquisitely the readjusted social attitudes it produced, when Mrs Elton (whose brother-in-law Mr Suckling has his fortune from Bristol) shows her over-sensitiveness on the subject by seeing a reference where none was made and replying 'if you mean a fling at the slave trade, I assure you Mr Suckling was always rather a friend to the abolition'. And a pervasive influence in *Mansfield Park*, mentioned explicitly only once (in Mary Crawford's sneer), is the challenge of Methodism to the serious people among the clergy of the Established Church.

Yet these direct references to contemporary conditions and events are a small part of Jane Austen's claim to a fundamentally serious concern with society. More important is her constant preoccupation with the moral basis of social relations, and the implicit judgment she passes on the social context of the experiences she shaped into entertainment.

Despite her manner of expecting from her readers a moral outlook and social good taste to match her own, she was far from feeling herself comfortably embedded in a society whose standards were acceptable to her. It is true that her novels were highly successful (and enjoyed by the Prince Regent among others) and that she lived an affectionate life with her family. But her work reveals, sometimes explicitly, sometimes more subtly, how little she supposed the greater part of her social world to live up to her standards of moral taste and cultivated intelligence. The possibility of holding a low opinion of people to whom one is bound by affection is stated in *Pride and Prejudice* as if it were a commonplace – in one of those scarcely noticed sentences of devastating implication which Jane Austen camouflages amidst more ordinarily acceptable or light-hearted remarks. Elizabeth is talking, half laughingly but with fundamental seriousness, to her sister Jane, who tries to think well of everybody: 'Do not be afraid of my running into any excess, of my encroaching on your privilege of universal goodwill. You need not. There are few people whom I really love, and still fewer of whom I think well.' A conflict of values between the heroine and her close associates, a conflict muted and generally known only to the heroine herself, is an intrinsic part of most of the novels, and because the heroine is also attached with genuine affection to those around her the tension is an inner one.

Romantic love gave Jane Austen a focus where individual values could achieve high definition, usually in conflict with the social code that condoned marriages for money and social standing. Such marriages were not just romantically distasteful, they were morally repugnant to Jane Austen. *Persuasion*, in some ways the most gravely reflective of the novels, deliberately states the obligation to treat love as the only allowable basis of marriage. The moral issue is summed up in Anne Elliot's discussion with her lover, to whom she has been reunited after the years that were lost to them when she gave in to the prudent persuasions of middle age and broke off her engagement. He tells her how afraid he had been that she might be persuaded into marrying her wealthy and highly eligible cousin by the same devoted godmother who had persuaded her to break her first engagement.

'You should have distinguished,' replied Anne. 'You should not have suspected me now; the case so different, and my age so different. If I was wrong in yielding to persuasion once, remember that it was to persuasion exerted on the side of safety, not of risk. When I yielded, I thought it was to duty; but no duty could be called in aid here. In marrying a man indifferent to me, all risk would have been incurred, and all duty violated.'

More lightly and ironically the same view is implied in *Mansfield Park* when the fashionably brought up Mary Crawford describes the situation of one of her smart friends.

'I look upon the Frasers to be about as unhappy as most other married people. And yet it was a most desirable match for Janet at the time. We were all delighted. She could not do otherwise than accept him, for he was rich, and she had nothing . . . Poor Janet has been sadly taken in; and yet there was nothing improper on her side; she did not run into the match inconsiderately, there was no want of foresight. She took three days to consider of his proposals; and during those three days asked the advice of everybody connected with her, whose opinion was worth having; and especially applied to my late dear aunt, whose knowledge of the world made her judgment very generally and deservedly looked up to by all the young people of her acquaintance; and she was decidedly in favour of Mr Fraser.'

The necessity to continue in amicable relations with one's associates in spite of holding essentially different standards is shown again and again in Jane Austen's work. For the heroine, it is true, the moral obligation to resist a loveless marriage may lead to actual conflict with her family, most notably in *Mansfield Park*. But equally the heroine must make the best of the fact that those to whom she is greatly attached may have no such standards. In *Pride and Prejudice* Elizabeth reflects on her friend Charlotte's marriage to Mr Collins solely in order to have an establishment of her own:

She had always felt that Charlotte's opinion of matrimony was not exactly like her own, but she could not have supposed it possible that, when called into action, she would have sacrificed every better feeling to worldly advantage.

But she retained this friend ('a friend disgracing herself and sunk in her esteem'), and came to feel a sort of respect for the self-control with which Charlotte tolerated her impossible husband and his patroness.

Although loyalty to the ideal of love between individuals was central to Jane Austen's social morality, she was reticent about their sexual attraction, taking it for granted as part of the total pattern of romantic love without giving it special emphasis. But she was far from being prudish or prim. Her cheerfully matter-of-fact attitude to child-birth, flippant once or twice in her letters, still shocks spinster minds, male and female. But bearing children was an everyday fact of social life, and she treated it without sentimentality or smirking, though well aware of the more usual quality of the gossip it provided; she refers, for instance, to 'the situation of Mrs Weston, whose happiness it was to be hoped might eventually be as much increased by the arrival of a child, as that of all her neighbours was by the approach of it.'

The novels make a similarly straightforward and entirely unprudish acknowledgement of loose sexual behaviour as an ordinary though deplorable human fact. Illegitimacy features in a matter-of-fact way in *Sense and Sensibility* and *Emma*; seduction and attempted seduction in *Sense and Sensibility* and *Pride and Prejudice* (with a duel fought on account of it in one and threatened in the other); adultery in *Mansfield Park*, and the open keeping of a mistress in *Mansfield Park* and *Persuasion*; and these things, though condemned, are taken as familiar, regrettable facts and never treated with a hush and a blush. Nor are the men and women who are guilty of them presented as monsters; most of them are well-bred, attractive members of polite society, with good qualities marred through faulty upbringing or mercenary marriage.

Her treatment of sexual attraction is in line with her general view that strong impulses and intensely emotional states should be regulated and controlled. *Sense and Sensibility*, of course, provides the simplest illustrations of the need for control and the refusal (on Marianne's part) to exert it. 'This violent oppression of spirits continued the whole evening. She was without any power, because she was without any desire of command over herself.' The control that Jane Austen respected was not to be exercized in favour of some abstract standard of 'reason', but in consideration for one's immediate companions. It fulfilled a social obligation, as Marianne shows in her self-reproaches after she has recovered from her serious illness, and as Mr Knightley implies when, sympathizing with what he supposes Emma to feel at the loss of Mr Frank Churchill, he says: 'Time, my dearest Emma, time will heal the wound. – Your own excellent sense – your exertions for your father's sake.' And again in *Pride and Prejudice*, concern for the effect of one's emotions on others ranks equal with good sense as a means of control:

> Having never fancied herself in love before, her regard had all the warmth of first attachment, and from her age and disposition, greater steadiness than first attachments often boast; and so fervently did she value his remembrance, and prefer him to every other man, that all her good sense, and all her attention to the feelings of her friends, were requisite to check the indulgence of those regrets which must have been injurious to her own health and their tranquillity.

Tumultuous experiences of any sort, joyful or disagreeable, have to be brought to order by private reflection until one is fit for society again, and the heroine's 'reflection' in her own room after a crisis or a climax is a usual feature of the novels. The importance of understanding and coming to terms with one's private feelings is never doubted; when that has been done, the heroine returns and takes her ordinary part in the commonplace of social intercourse. The separation of important private feelings from the routine of social behaviour, even amidst the family and its close associates, not only safeguards the comfort of others but allows the heroine's personal judgment to establish itself and secures her own moral autonomy. Moral autonomy is a striking feature of Jane Austen's heroines; although she never fails to pay tribute to the vital importance of sound upbringing and the early inculcation of good principles, yet her heroines are always required to make sounder judgments than those around them (including their parents) or like Emma, to correct their errors through their own experience and not through submission to the advice of others.

She makes this autonomy of judgment possible, in spite of the close pressure of society, by imagining for her heroines a social context in which indifference, impercipience, or considerate reticence allow their feelings on important matters to be very little known even to their near associates. Closely as the sisters of *Sense and Sensibility* and of *Pride and Prejudice* are attached to each other, great reticence is maintained between them. And when the Gardiners, Elizabeth Bennet's civilized uncle and aunt, observe with astonishment Darcy's attentions to her, she hurries away 'fearful of enquiries or hints':

> But she had no reason to fear Mr and Mrs Gardiner's curiosity; it was not their wish to force her communication. It was evident that she was much better acquainted with Mr Darcy than they had before any

idea of; it was evident that he was very much in love with her. They saw much to interest, but nothing to justify enquiry.

This is the positive ideal that she sets over against the prying intrusions of Mrs Jennings in *Sense and Sensibility*. And in *Persuasion* Anne and Lady Russell, in spite of their intimate and affectionate relation, have never in seven years alluded to the broken engagement, and Lady Russell has no knowledge of what Anne may feel about her former lover. Jane Austen was here no doubt exaggerating and idealizing current conventions of her society. The effect was to make possible for her heroines a striking degree of private judgment (and often condemnation) of conventional values while still preserving outward amenability.

Not only do her heroines maintain the forms of politeness to those they dislike, as Emma so scrupulously does with Mrs Elton, but they may be detached even from their close friends by private reservations and conceal-ments. Emma, for example, finds that her party to Box Hill is to be spoilt by the inclusion of the intolerable Mrs Elton at the invitation of Emma's thoroughly amiable friend Mr Weston, who hopes she has no objection.

Now, as her objection was nothing but her very great dislike of Mrs Elton, of which Mr Weston must already be perfectly aware, it was not worth bringing forward again: – it could not be done without a reproof to him, which would be giving pain to his wife; and she found herself therefore obliged to consent to an arrangement which she would have done a great deal to avoid; an arrangement which would probably expose her even to the degradation of being said to be of Mrs Elton's party! Every feeling was offended; and the forbearance of her outward submission left a heavy arrear due of secret severity in her reflections on the unmanageable good-will of Mr Weston's temper.

'I am glad you approve of what I have done,' said he very comfortably. But I thought you would. Such schemes as these are nothing without numbers. One cannot have too large a party. A large party secures its own amusement. And she is a good-natured woman after all. One could not leave her out.'

Emma denied none of it aloud, and agreed to none of it in private.

This kind of tension between the woman of genuine good taste and moral fastidiousness and even those to whom she is sincerely attached is characteristic of Jane Austen's work. *Emma*, which shows polite concealment carried very far, also shows the dilemma it creates for those who value sincerity but know that a frank definition of their own values would seem a slight or a reproof to many of their friends. When Frank Churchill professes to be 'the wretchedest being in the world at a civil falsehood', '"I do not believe any such thing," replied Emma. "I am persuaded that you can be as insincere as your neighbours, when it is necessary."' And the full significance of the exchange depends on the fact that Frank Churchill is at this very time occupied in acting out with the utmost skill a serious falsehood by which Emma herself is being thoroughly taken in. So, too, there is an ironic contrast between Emma's own readiness for keeping her opinions to herself and her great dislike of Jane Fairfax's 'reserve'; it is Emma, so skilled in holding her tongue, who exclaims to Jane, when the disclosure of the secret engagement makes reserve no longer necessary, 'Thank you, thank you. – This is just what I wanted to be assured of. Oh! if you know how much I love everything that is decided and open!' Early in the book she supposes that after his

marriage Mr Elton has made Harriet's ill-starred infatuation for him 'a sacrifice to conjugal unreserve'. But at the
end of the book Emma looks forward with relief to
Harriet's marriage with her farmer so that she herself can
at last give up the reserve she has had to maintain with her
own husband-to-be about Harriet's affairs. The inconsistencies, whether or not intended as deliberate ironies by
Jane Austen, point to the dilemma of a subtle and sensitive
woman who had to come to terms with the moral and
intellectual mediocrity of a society on which she was
dependent and of friends and relations with whom she
had the closest and most affectionate ties. The detachment
and autonomy of the individual as a centre of self-
responsible moral judgment, which she maintained
unswervingly, was in fact another variant of that reaction
against submission to ready-made social codes which marks
Blake, Shelley, Wordsworth, and even Byron.

CHAPTER 5

Character and Caricature in Jane Austen

It seems abundantly clear that in reading Jane Austen's novels we are not intended to take all the figures in the same way. Some are offered as full and natural portraits of imaginable people; others while certainly referring to types of people we might easily have come across are yet presented with such exaggeration and simplification that our response to them is expected to be rather different. When Mr Collins has annoyed Mrs Bennet by supposing that one of her daughters has helped with the cooking:

> He begged pardon for having displeased her. In a softened tone she declared herself not at all offended; but he continued to apologize for about a quarter of an hour.

If we were to object that this surely is rather unlikely – two or three minutes perhaps but hardly a quarter of an hour – it would be a misreading; we should be missing the fact that this is a convention of joking exaggeration. We accept the same convention when we read in *Sense and Sensibility* of Charlotte's meaningless laughter. They arrived at her home and spent the rest of the morning:

> in dawdling through the greenhouse, where the loss of her favourite plants, unwarily exposed, and nipped by the lingering frost, raised the laughter of Charlotte – and in visiting her poultry-yard, where, in the disappointed hopes of her dairymaid, by hens forsaking their nests, or being stolen by a fox, or in the rapid decease

of a promising young brood, she found fresh sources of merriment.

In Charlotte, besides exaggeration, there is the device, used so much by Dickens, of the label tagged on and frequently repeated. Of other figures it may be the preliminary description which assures us that some trait of personality is being as sharply and mockingly emphasized as the nose or eyebrows of a politician in a cartoon. Thus the initial account of Sir Walter Elliot's vanity about his rank and personal appearance concludes:

> He considered the blessing of beauty as inferior only to the blessing of a baronetcy; and the Sir Walter Elliot who united these gifts was the constant object of his warmest respect and devotion.

Here it is the tone of ironic mockery in describing a defect of personality that announces the intention of caricature.

The natural portraiture which contrasts with this sort of treatment is of course a relative matter. All character portrayal is selective, involving the accentuation of some features; and it produces, inevitably, an effect more condensed and more tidily organized than the impression we gain of a real companion in the undramatic and haphazard contacts of everyday life. But great selective emphasis can be consistent with the author's intention of offering a credible portrait. Elizabeth Bennet's angelic sister Jane is certainly meant to be taken seriously as a character even though her wish to think well of everybody is heightened to the point of becoming a joke, as for instance when she hears from Elizabeth of the bad feeling between Darcy and Wickham. Greatly troubled she casts about for some way of clearing them both:

> 'They have both', said she, 'been deceived, I dare say, in some way or other of which we can form no

idea. Interested people have perhaps misrepresented each to the other. It is, in short, impossible for us to conjecture the causes or circumstances which may have alienated them without actual blame on either side.'

And Elizabeth replies ironically:

'Very true, indeed; – and now, my dear Jane, what have you got to say in behalf of the interested people who have probably been concerned in the business? – Do clear them too, or we shall be obliged to think ill of somebody.'

We can go further and notice that sometimes a characteristic may be carried to implausible excess without any intention of caricature. Fanny Price's meek piety is so overdone as to verge on unacceptable priggishness, but we see this as a misjudgment in the handling of a portrait, not the result of deliberate caricature. What matters is a tacit understanding between author and reader as to which technique of presentation is being adopted.

It hardly needs saying that transitional forms may occur on the borderline between character and caricature, and there is occasionally a mixture of the two techniques in one figure, a possibility that must be examined later. Broadly, however, the difference of treatment is plain enough. It can be exemplified by the contrast between, say, Mr Collins and Wickham in *Pride and Prejudice*, between Mrs Jennings and Lucy Steele in *Sense and Sensibility*, between Mrs Elton and Harriet Smith in *Emma*, between Mrs Norris and Mrs Grant in *Mansfield Park*, or between Sir Walter Elliot and Mr Elliot in *Persuasion*. These are all fairly subordinate figures. If instead we compare the heroes or heroines with the caricatures, for instance Elizabeth Bennet with Mr Collins or Mr Knightly with Miss Bates, the difference of handling amounts to a sharp antithesis. The question then arises how such very diverse treatments of the figures can be successfully combined in the one work. Certainly in painting it must be rather rare for caricature and full portraiture to be brought together in one group. And the further possibility arises that besides creating problems the diversity of treatment in a single novel may also present an opportunity for effects that could otherwise not be achieved.

We can best approach these questions by taking a further look at the methods by which Jane Austen tacitly conveys to us that a figure is going to be treated as caricature. At the beginning of *Mansfield Park*, after one or two ironic comments, suggestive but not conclusive, on Mrs Norris's anger and spirit of activity, an unmistakeable indication that she is to be caricature appears in the long speech with which she interrupts Sir Thomas to reply to all the hesitations, whether stated or not, which he may feel about taking Fanny Price into his home. Her arguments are sensible enough, the phrasing not silly, but the speech is so disproportionate in length and dogmatic certainty to Sir Thomas's attempt at cautious consideration that we recognize at once the volubility of the opinionated and domineering woman who goes over other people like a steam roller. The long speech, in which she expects and receives no help from social give and take, creates the impression that she is being exhibited and exposed. The stage is set for ridicule. And a little later comes the revelation that she has no intention of having a child in her own house, preceded by an explicit statement, rather in the style of the seventeenth century 'character', of one of the traits which is to be ridiculed throughout the novel:

> As far as walking, talking, and contriving reached, she was thoroughly benevolent, and nobody knew better how to dictate liberality to others: but her love of money was equal to her love of directing, and she

knew quite as well how to save her own as to spend
that of her friends.

The contrast between ostensible generosity and mean
intentions could easily have been presented as one aspect
of a real and rather similar character. Mrs Norris is seen to
be caricature because of the repetition of her exaggerated
claims to selfless benevolence, the transparently spurious
reason she offers for her refusal (selfless devotion again –
to her husband's health), and the technique of self-
exhibition in lengthy, uninterrupted speeches. Whether
or not that technique derives from the early novels in
letter form there is no doubt that it follows on easily from
them; Lady Susan, for example, fully exposes her own
character in the first two letters.

It is at all events a frequent feature of Jane Austen's
presentation of her caricatures. Mrs Elton's first visit to
Hartfield displays it. She is given long speeches comparing
Hartfield to Maple Grove and singing the praises of Bath
and Jane Fairfax, and here again the substance of what she
said could have formed part of a full portrait, not a
caricature, of a pushing and ill-judging woman. But in
that case it would have had to be incorporated into
genuine conversation, related effectively to what the other
person said. In fact Emma is given only the briefest replies,
mostly to keep her visitor at arm's length, and the effect is
to leave Mrs Elton conversing. With Mrs Norris the
replies of the other people are at least briefly given; with
Miss Bates they are sometimes omitted entirely, even
though it may be indicated that some brief word has been
got in edgeways, and we have such openly exaggerated
displays as the famous speech on her arrival for the ball at
the Crown:

'So very obliging of you! No rain at all. Nothing to
signify. I do not care for myself. Quite thick shoes. And

Jane declares – Well!' (as soon as she was within the door), 'well! This is brilliant indeed! This is admirable! Excellently contrived, upon my word. Nothing wanting. Could not have imagined it. So well lighted up! Jane, Jane, look! did you ever see anything – Oh! Mr Weston, you must really have had Aladdin's lamp. Good Mrs Stokes would not know her own room again. I saw her as I came in; she was standing in the entrance. "Oh! Mrs Stokes," said I – but I had not time for more.' She was now met by Mrs Weston. 'Very well, I thank you ma'am. I hope you are quite well. Very happy to hear it. So afraid you might have a headache! seeing you pass by so often, and knowing how much trouble you must have. Delighted to hear it indeed! – Ah! dear Mrs Elton, so obliged to you for the carriage; excellent time; Jane and I quite ready. Did not keep the horses a moment. Most comfortable carriage.'

And so it goes on and on. In this and many of her speeches Miss Bates is labelled as a caricature largely by being displayed against non-contributing listeners. Real characters may have long speeches, sometimes too long and prosy, like some of Elinor's and Marianne's during the latter's convalescence, but they are none the less offered as part of a true conversational interchange. The caricature of the domineering or talkative person is largely secured by eliminating any response that could establish social interchange. At its extreme we have the frankly foreshortened and non-realistic representation of Mrs Elton gathering strawberries, where her continuous talk is reduced to jottings:*

Mrs Elton in all her apparatus of happiness, her large bonnet and her basket, was very ready to lead the way in

---

* It may be that the jottings represent the conversation of the whole party, though Mary Lascelles takes Mrs Elton to be the speaker; she is at least the dominant speaker.

gathering, accepting, or talking. Strawberries, and only strawberries, could now be thought or spoken of. 'The best fruit in England – everybody's favourite – always wholesome. These are the finest beds and finest sorts. Delightful to gather for one's self – the only way of really enjoying them. Morning decidedly the best time – never tired – every sort good – hautboy infinitely superior – no comparison – the others hardly eatable – hautboys very scarce – Chili preferred – white wood finest flavour of all – price of strawberries in London – abundance about Bristol – Maple Grove – cultivation – beds when to be renewed – gardeners thinking exactly different – no general rule – gardeners never to be put out of their way – delicious fruit – only too rich to be eaten much of – inferior to cherries – currants more refreshing – only objection to gathering strawberries the stooping – glaring sun – tired to death – could bear it no longer – must go and sit in the shade.'

Such, for half an hour, was the conversation; interrupted only once by Mrs Weston, who came out, in her solicitude after her son-in-law, to inquire if he were come.

The effect of thus cutting away the social background is to make the figure literally egregious. It is what Jane Austen does in first bringing Robert Ferrars on to the scene and establishing him as a caricature of a coxcomb. Elinor and Marianne, who have no idea who he is, simply wait their turn to be attended to at the jewellers while he perpetrates a display of puppyism in choosing his toothpick case:

At last the affair was decided. The ivory, the gold, and the pearls, all received their appointment, and the gentlemen having named the last day on which his existence could be continued without the possession of the toothpick-case, drew on his gloves with leisurely

care, and bestowing another glance on the Miss Dash-
woods, but such a one as seemed rather to demand than
to express admiration, walked off with an happy air of
real conceit and affected indifference.

It constitutes a performance in front of us, and in front of
the sisters, without the mitigation of any personal contact,
leaving him a ridiculous object rather than a social person.

By means such as these, among others, Jane Austen
announces, and from time to time reiterates, that a figure is
meant to be taken as caricature. The early presentation of
these caricatures differs totally from that of a figure like
Harriet Smith, who is presented as shy and naive and at first
out of place when she visits Hartfield, and is exposed to
our laughter at later points in the novel, but is still offered
as a character. Her speeches are always part of a true
conversational interchange, and her absurdity (such as her
treasuring up laughably trivial mementoes of Mr Elton)
arises out of her particularized experience in the story and
is not tacked on to her as if it were one of the identifying
tags by which she is to be recognized.

With the tacit understanding established that a figure is
caricature the reader is prepared for certain differences in
its handling. As a general rule attention is then concentrated
on a few features or a small segment of the personality to
the neglect of much that would make the figure a full
human being, and the understanding is that the reader will
accept this convention and not inquire closely into the
areas of behaviour and personality that the author chooses
to avoid. In this respect caricature is one of many conventions in entertainment and communication. It can be compared in its artificiality with the funny anecdote; the listener
who, at the improbable climax of a joke, is so unco-
operative as to inquire 'Well, and what happened *then*?' or
'What did he say to *that*?' has failed to play his part in the
convention which frames off the incident from any real

context. In its technique of isolating and exaggerating a few traits, caricature has affinities also with the stereotyped thinking that provides figures like the gay, gesticulating, amorous Frenchman, the correct and inhibited Englishman with tightly rolled umbrella, or the spinster in old-fashioned clothes devoted to her cat. Stereotypes serve limited purposes of communication and comment, they may convey elements of true generalization, but they work only because of an implicit agreement to ignore the greater part of any real personality in which the exaggerated features are embedded. In fiction, similarly, caricature will work so long as the reader accepts the bargain and so long as no important action which would be impossible to a more complete personality is made to hinge on the exaggerated feature. The incompleteness of the caricature is due largely to a restriction in the kinds of situation in which he is allowed to appear. Mrs Jennings is easily maintained as a caricature while she is no more than a gossiping member of casual parties; once she is involved in such situations as Marianne's serious illness she gains another dimension and for a time the air of caricature is very much lessened.

It is of course a further mark of the caricatures that they are in some degree ridiculous, proper targets for laughter that has an element of hostility or condemnation. The fact of its being *laughing* condemnation implies that in some sense we write them off as not seriously mattering. That, however, is a difficult statement to sustain unless we discriminate between the reader's view and the view taken by characters in the fiction. For example, so long as Elizabeth Bennet can see Mr Collins with contemptuous amusement *our* view of him as a caricature and *her* view of him as – within the fictional world – a real person are not noticeably different. When, however, he proposes to Elizabeth, and her mother's urgent pressure turns the proposal into a genuine threat, then we have to recognize that although he remains a joke for us he has become no joke for her. Nor is he a joke for her when Charlotte Lucas marries him. The handling of him as a caricature is a convention between author and readers; the other fictional figures are not party to it. Again, Lady Catherine in the shrubbery, forbidding Elizabeth to become engaged to Darcy, touches the heights of caricature for us:

> 'Heaven and earth! – of what are you thinking? Are the shades of Pemberley to be thus polluted?'

But for Elizabeth she is a threat, a very real person; Elizabeth for her own part can confidently judge her to be absurd, but at the same time her power, especially over Darcy, is not easily gauged:

> She knew not the exact degree of his affection for his aunt, or his dependence on her judgment, but it was natural to suppose that he thought much higher of her ladyship than *she* could do.

When we think of Mrs Norris and Fanny Price it is inescapable that the figure which *we* are invited to ridicule can certainly be no laughing matter to the heroine. The technique of caricature constitutes communication on a different level between the author and her readers. It assures us that although the heroine may be distressed and in a material sense endangered by the caricatured figure the danger and trouble will always remain external, the threat will not be to the values which make her the heroine. The fully portrayed characters, on the other hand, have a much more intimate relevance to her. Henry Crawford's wooing of Fanny, and the pressures exerted in his favour by Sir Thomas and Edmund, are serious not only to her but to us: his success would change the whole pattern of values to

which we have committed ourselves in sympathizing with
the heroine. The same is true of Mr Elliot's wooing of
Anne.

With a genial caricature like Admiral Croft the case is
slightly different because we and the heroine see him in the
same light. But like all caricatures, he is external to her; he
is distanced, and in spite of his fundamental goodness he
has little connection with her more intimate values. He can
contribute agreeably to casual social intercourse but no
more. It was one of the weaknesses of the cancelled chapter
of *Persuasion* that the impulsive action of a caricature figure
was made crucial in securing the union of the hero and
heroine; the revision brought the union about, instead,
through interaction on the level of their most serious values
and with the involvement of Captain Harville, who is a
subordinate character but not a caricature. Anne's decisive
talk with Captain Harville within hearing of Captain Wentworth is an example of the true conversational interchange, neither person detached or superior, which marks
characters and cannot occur between a character and a
caricature. It is part of the understanding between author
and reader that the figures we accept as caricature cannot
have full social relevance to the characters. Even Mrs Croft
treats her husband with some degree of clinical detachment. As they drive home in their gig the Admiral remarks:

'I wish Frederick would spread a little more canvas,
and bring us home one of these young ladies to Kellynch.
Then, there would always be company for them. – And
very nice young ladies they both are; I hardly know one
from the other.'

'Very good humoured, unaffected girls, indeed,' said
Mrs Croft, in a tone of calmer praise, such as made Anne
suspect that her keener powers might not consider either
of them as quite worthy of her brother; 'and a very
respectable family. One could not be connected with

better people. – My dear admiral, that post! – we shall certainly take that post.'

But by coolly giving the reins a better direction herself, they happily passed the danger; and by once afterwards judiciously putting out her hand, they neither fell into a rut, nor ran foul of a dung-cart; and Anne, with some amusement at their style of driving, which she imagined no bad representation of the general guidance of their affairs, found herself safely deposited by them at the cottage.

There is in fact a close relation between the handling of a fictional figure as caricature and the clinical attitude that we adopt in real life towards someone who is drunk, very ignorant, irritable with tiredness, or in some other way less than an equal companion. We have to pull our punches. Our forbearance, justifiable though it may be, reduces his interpersonal status; his actions are no longer allowed full social relevance, we belittle him by humouring him.

This may be seen in *Emma*. Mr Woodhouse must be regarded at least in part as caricature (though he is perhaps a transitional figure). We consequently accept without much difficulty Emma's humouring of him and the affectionate manipulation that reduces him almost to the status of a child. About Harriet Smith we feel differently. With all her limitations she is presented as a character, a full portrait, and it is an offence on Emma's part to manipulate her and reduce her personhood by managing her affections for her.

To see rather more clearly how a character and a caricature are differentiated it is instructive to watch the developing presentation of the two Steele sisters in *Sense and Sensibility* after their simultaneous entry into the novel. At first they are potential caricatures while they flatter Lady Middleton by their improbable delight and excessive patience with her intolerably spoiled children. But while the treatment of the elder Miss Steele continues along the line of caricature, simplified and exaggerated, Lucy is made more complex; her greater intelligence and subtlety are quickly demonstrated when she hints that she perfectly appreciates Elinor's juster estimate of the children and wants to reconcile her own behaviour with it:

> 'I have a notion,' said Lucy, 'you think the little Middletons rather too much indulged; perhaps they may be the outside of enough; but it is so natural in Lady Middleton; and for my part, I love to see children full of life and spirits; I cannot bear them if they are quiet and tame.'

Soon afterwards when her elder sister has displayed her vulgarity in her discussion of 'smart beaux', which Lucy translates into 'genteel young men', Lucy is again detached from her by being given a little more awareness of Elinor's outlook.

> 'Lord! Anne,' cried her sister, 'you can talk of nothing but beaux; – you will make Miss Dashwood believe you think of nothing else.'

There soon follows the private talk in which Lucy – under colour of confiding in another woman whose discretion she trusts – warns Elinor off Edward Ferrars by revealing her own secret engagement to him. In the talks that follow she is shown to be insincere and cunning, but the disclosure of these traits is associated so closely with the particular facts of her relations with Edward and Elinor, that she begins to be a unique person in a unique situation and not, like her elder sister, a sketched outline with salient features that could belong to any one of hundreds of vulgar and opportunist women.

It is not a fictional figure's own behaviour and remarks that decide whether we see him as caricature or character; the behaviour he elicits from the fully drawn characters also counts. Miss Steele, the elder sister, gets very little response from Elinor. The most notable is Elinor's shock on discovering that Miss Steele's account of a conversation between Lucy Steele and Edward Ferrars is based on eavesdropping, and then Elinor's reply is little beyond the copy-book propriety that Jane Austen too often gives her.

Lucy Steele's quality as a full character is conveyed partly through the sharply felt and sometimes unexpected reactions she provokes in Elinor. In their tête-à-tête, while they work on a filigree basket for Lady Middleton's spoilt Annamaria, Lucy affirms her conviction of Edward Ferrar's continuing attachment and Elinor, knowing that she herself has become the object of his love and that Lucy suspects it, replies:

> 'If the strength of your reciprocal attachment had failed, as between many people and under many circumstances it naturally would during a four years' engagement, your situation would have been pitiable indeed.'
>
> Lucy here looked up; but Elinor was careful in guarding her countenance from every expression that could give her words a suspicious tendency.

A little later Lucy expatiates on her certainty that if Edward had shown the least sign of wavering in his attachment she could not have failed to detect it. "'All this,' thought Elinor, 'is very pretty; but it can impose upon neither of us.'"

So the covert duel goes on, Lucy steadily and solemnly affirming her tender attachment to Edward and her certainty of his to her; and the effect of her protestations is that:

Elinor sat down to the card table with the melancholy persuasion that Edward was not only without affection for the person who was to be his wife; but that he had not even the chance of being tolerably happy in marriage, which sincere affection on *her* side would have given, for self-interest alone could induce a woman to keep a man to an engagement, of which she seemed so thoroughly aware that he was weary.

Elinor's detached distrust and this cynical conclusion give an extra dimension to the preceding dialogue and add depth to the figure of Lucy.

The elder Miss Steele by contrast remains a fairly conventional cardboard figure. Soon after she has served her purpose by blurting out the news of Lucy's secret engagement and producing uproar among the Ferrars's she is eased off the scene. Her last appearance is in Kensington Gardens where she serves to bring news of Lucy's determination to retain her hold on Edward, and after a little joyful anticipation of being teased about the doctor she departs with the assurance that she and Lucy are very ready to accept any invitations that may come their way.

> 'and if anything should happen to take you and your sister away, and Mrs Jennings should want company, I am sure we should be very glad to come and stay with her for as long a time as she likes. I suppose Lady Middleton won't ask us any more this bout. Good-bye; I am sorry Miss Marianne was not here. Remember me kindly to her. La! if you have not got your spotted muslin on! I wonder you was not afraid of its being torn.'

We see her no more and almost at the end of the book merely hear of Mrs Jennings's good nature in giving her five guineas to get her back to Exeter when Lucy has borrowed all her money and left her stranded. The puppet has been put back into its box.

And towards the ending of the novels this happens to most of the exaggerated figures. As the 'real people' are drawn more closely together the caricatures are removed to a greater distance and come in only as echoes. It is a device that contributes crucially to the tone of the ending; the serious sentiment which is fundamental in Jane Austen's structure of values might be too much of a contrast, or might even be cloying, if it were offered neat and concentrated at the end. Echoes from the caricatures aerate and lighten it. Mrs Jennings's letter most dexterously and briefly recapitulates her own good nature, her vulgar and almost mechanical willingness to tease girls about their lovers, Miss Steele's cadging of hospitality, and her craving to be thought still in the running for marriage:

> 'Lucy, it seems, borrowed all her money before she went off to be married, on purpose, we suppose, to make a show with, and poor Nancy had not seven shillings in the world; so I was very glad to give her five guineas to take her down to Exeter, where she thinks of staying three or four weeks with Mrs Burgess, in hopes, as I tell her, to fall in with the doctor again.'

The final paragraph of *Emma* exemplifies the same device:

> 'The wedding was very much like other weddings, where the parties have no taste for finery or parade; and Mrs Elton, from the particulars detailed by her husband, thought it all extremely shabby, and very inferior to her own. "Very little white satin, very few lace veils; a most pitiful business! Selina would stare when she heard of it." But, in spite of these deficiencies, the wishes, the hopes, the confidence, the predictions of the small band

of true friends who witnessed the ceremony, were fully
answered in the perfect happiness of the union.'

Mrs Elton's comments, with the preceding reference to
the avoidance of finery and parade, brings back to mind
her dinner visit at Hartfield and her comment to Jane
Fairfax on Mr Woodhouse's politeness:

> 'I fancy I am rather a favourite; he took notice of my
> gown. How do you like it? – Selina's choice – handsome,
> I think, but I do not know whether it is not over-
> trimmed; I have the greatest dislike to the idea of being
> over-trimmed; – quite a horror of finery. I must put on
> a few ornaments *now*, because it is expected of me. A
> bride, you know, must appear like a bride, but my
> natural taste is all for simplicity; a simple style of dress is
> so infinitely preferable to finery. But I am quite in the
> minority, I believe; few people seem to value simplicity
> of dress – show and finery are everything. I have some
> notion of putting such a trimming as this to my white
> and silver poplin. Do you think it will look well?'

And there is a similar passage before the ball at the Crown
– '"How do you like my gown? How do you like my
trimming? – How has Wright done my hair? . . . I see very
few pearls in the room except mine."' All of this is
recapitulated in the last brief echo.

The necessity for fading out or modifying the caricatures
towards the end of the novel is one aspect of a general
problem: how can contacts between characters and caricatures be managed without creating an unacceptable incongruity? At times the incongruity is too evident and the
transition between the two sorts of treatment seems clumsy.
To my mind an instance occurs in *Pride and Prejudice* when
the Bennets, distressed by Lydia's elopement and probable

ruin, sit down to dinner, and Mary, indefatigable in stale and stilted moral reflections, remarks to Elizabeth:

> 'This is a most unfortunate affair, and will probably be much talked of. But we must stem the tide of malice, and pour into the wounded bosoms of each other the balm of sisterly consolation.'

Then perceiving in Elizabeth no inclination of replying, she added, 'Unhappy as the event must be for Lydia, we may draw from it this useful lesson: that loss of virtue in a female is irretrievable, that one false step involves her in endless ruin, that her reputation is no less brittle than it is beautiful, and that she cannot be too much guarded in her behaviour towards the undeserving of the other sex.'

Elizabeth lifted up her eyes in amazement, but was too much oppressed to make any reply. Mary, however, continued to console herself with such kind of moral extractions from the evil before them.

The passage of caricature comes in rather abruptly at that point, and Elizabeth's reaction provides a less smooth junction between the two techniques than Jane Austen usually manages. Associating Elizabeth and Jane with the largely caricatural figures of some members of the family creates a problem which she usually solves by keeping the two elder sisters quiet while the caricatures exhibit, as she does when the two elder sisters, on their way home from London, are met by Lydia and Catherine who have ordered a meal for them at an inn and entertain them with a noisy account of their folly. Jane and Elizabeth, though present, are in the audience, almost as much spectators as we are, and largely keeping their thoughts to themselves.

Pride and Prejudice, however, stands a little apart from the other novels in a certain stageyness of technique which suggests the influence of the theatre. The dialogue is often crisply theatrical in quality. Jane assures Elizabeth, without any success, that she no longer loves Bingley or supposes him to love her, and there follows what could well be stage dialogue:

> 'You are very cruel,' said her sister; 'you will not let me smile, and are provoking me to it every moment.'
> 'How hard it is in some cases to be believed!'
> 'And how impossible in others!'
> 'But why should you wish to persuade me that I feel more than I acknowledge?'
> 'That is a question which I hardly know how to answer. We all love to instruct, though we can teach only what is not worth knowing. Forgive me; and if you persist in indifference, do not make *me* your confidante.'

And when Mr Bennet has been called on to compel Elizabeth to marry Mr Collins his speech works up to a climax that demands laughter from an audience:

> 'Come here, child,' cried her father, as she appeared. 'I have sent for you on an affair of importance. I understand that Mr Collins has made you an offer of marriage. Is it true?' Elizabeth replied that it was. 'Very well. And this offer of marriage you have refused?'
> 'I have, sir.'
> 'Very well. We now come to the point. Your mother insists upon your accepting it. – Is it not so, Mrs Bennet?'
> 'Yes, or I will never see her again.'
> 'An unhappy alternative is before you, Elizabeth. From this day you must be a stranger to one of your parents. Your mother will never see you again if you do *not* marry Mr Collins, and I will never see you again if you *do*.'

Laughter from an auditorium would carry the scene forward, but there is something of a drop in the continuity passage which actually follows:

> Elizabeth could not but smile at such a conclusion of such a beginning; but Mrs Bennet, who had persuaded herself that her husband regarded the affair as she wished, was excessively disappointed.

Several other scenes, conducted mainly in dialogue, have the quality of set pieces: for instance Mr Collins's proposal, Mr Darcy's first proposal, Lady Catherine and Elizabeth confronting each other in the little wilderness. In scenes like this there is a suggestion of stage dialogue which contrasts with the greater naturalness of conversation and indirectly reported speech in Mr Darcy's second proposal or in Elizabeth's interview with her father after Darcy has asked his consent. In these latter scenes the technique of the novel is in control. But the influence of the eighteenth century theatre in some parts of the novel is consistent with the very strongly marked caricature of some figures and a rather sharp transition from them to the seriously portrayed characters.

Where the technique of the novelist is dominant, as it is for the greater part of the later novels, the contacts between characters and caricatures are handled more smoothly. In *Emma* Jane Fairfax presents a considerable problem owing to her being in effective contact for the greater part of the story almost exclusively with Miss Bates and Mrs Elton, both caricatures. The solution is to minimize her contribution, to use her mainly as a foil, and to have her merits described rather than displayed. Thus when Mrs Elton at the ball pays her 'a good many compliments on her dress and look' we know nothing of her reply except that they were 'compliments very quietly and properly taken'. When we do hear some sustained interchange between them about securing a position for Jane as a governess a sort of dislocation occurs in the conversation. Jane herself, in her horror of being a governess, becomes the one who holds forth in exaggerated terms. Mrs Elton insists that they must begin at once to seek a post for her, and Jane replies:

> 'Excuse me, ma'am, but this is by no means my intention; I make no inquiry myself, and should be sorry to have any made by my friends. When I am quite determined as to the time, I am not at all afraid of being long unemployed. There are places in town, offices, where inquiry would soon produce something – offices for the sale, not quite of human flesh, but of human intellect.'
>
> 'Oh! my dear, human flesh! You quite shock me; if you mean a fling at the slave trade, I assure you Mr Suckling was always rather a friend to the abolition.'
>
> 'I did not mean – I was not thinking of the slave-trade,' replied Jane; 'governess-trade, I assure you, was all that I had in view; widely different, certainly, as to the guilt of those who carry it on; but as to the greater misery of the victims, I do not know where it lies.'

The dialogue here is unusual in making the character almost outdo the caricature in exaggerated emphasis.

Towards the end of *Emma* Jane Austen brings together her caricature, Mrs Elton, and her two characters, Jane Fairfax and Emma, in the scene in which Emma tries to convey her good wishes on Jane's engagement and Jane tries to indicate her appreciation but both are frustrated by Mrs Elton's obtrusive indication that she and Jane alone are in the secret of the engagement. The caricature is given her head for most of the scene and then Jane Austen takes Emma and Jane out on to the stairs and there the two characters have the brief but effective interchange that puts them in touch with each other and assures us that the distance and misunderstanding between them have been overcome.

It would be going much too far to imply that characters and caricatures are never brought into full contact, with both sides actively contributing. The scenes between Elizabeth and Lady Catherine, both at Rosings and at Longbourne, testify that they can be. But it seems rare for there to be an equal contribution from both figures when one is a portrait and the other a caricature. The more usual contact is represented by Miss Bates talking through the window to Mr Knightly, or Anne Elliot walking up the street in Bath with Admiral Croft and hearing his account of Louisa's engagement to Captain Benwick. The character in such interchanges generally says much less and also occupies a superior position – superior in terms of the values implied by the novel – to some extent humouring the other.

At other points the interaction between the two modes of presentation secures special effects in the communication that goes on between author and readers. Thus the handling of Mrs Norris assures us from the start how awful she is, but Sir Thomas, handled as a character, is supposed to be taken in by her, not unaware of her peculiarities but believing her to be guided by fundamentally sound principles and good intentions. The caricature brings out to us what is supposed to be hidden from him and consequently makes a limiting comment on the ponderous rationality which for him takes the place of insight. In this respect, one can argue, the technique of caricature allows Jane Austen to express what a person of her acute insight must always feel – astonishment at the way the most outrageously deformed personalities are allowed an effective part in society, because society attends seriously to lip service and rationalization. It is against the blindness and injustice of such a society that Fanny Price is finally vindicated. Rather more subtly Jane Austen insists on the reality of the mon-

strous Mr Collins in two ways: first by showing the real
pressure that Mrs Bennet exerted to make Elizabeth marry
him; and second, and more thoughtfully, by allowing him
to secure Charlotte, a real person, and letting Elizabeth
gradually realize, after the first shock of horror, that her
friend was after all making a tolerable life for herself in the
second-best world that most people except heroines have
to inhabit.

Caricature is maintained by concentrating on the outer
layers of social behaviour and selecting narrowly even from
them. In the same way that national stereotypes partly
dissolve when we come to know a foreigner as a real
person, so fictional caricatures may be given fuller human
relevance as the outer layers are penetrated and less grotesque features of personality are indicated. It is not only
Marianne but we too who have to enlarge our view of Mrs
Jennings to give a juster estimate of her good nature. We
are taken beyond the Lady Bertram of needlework and pug
when she is shocked into genuine feeling at the sight of her
son Tom desperately ill. But it is in Miss Bates that Jane
Austen exploits most delicately the technique of going
behind the ridiculous features of the caricature. What she
does, more than once, is unexpectedly to give Miss Bates
the moral advantage in a social situation, with the effect of
taking down a peg those – including us – who have felt
comfortably superior to her. This happens on the occasion
when Frank Churchill makes his blunder by revealing that
Mr Perry had intended to set up his carriage. Miss Bates
shoulders responsibility for the leakage of the story, which
Mrs Perry has told Mrs Bates in confidence:

'she had no objection to her telling us, of course, but
it was not to go beyond: and, from that day to this, I
never mentioned it to a soul that I know of. At the same
time, I will not positively answer for my having never
dropt a hint, because I know I do sometimes pop out a

thing before I am aware. I am a talker, you know; I am rather a talker; and now and then I have let a thing escape me which I should not. I am not like Jane; I wish I were. I will answer for it *she* never betrayed the least thing in the world.'

Frank Churchill and Jane know, as we know later, that he got the story through their clandestine correspondence. Miss Bates, honestly admitting her weakness, which this time is not to blame, leaves us feeling a little small. A similar effect is secured when Emma calls on the Bates's and, being admitted too promptly, sees Jane hurry into her bedroom to escape her:

and, before the door had shut them out, she heard Miss Bates saying, 'Well, my dear, I shall *say* you are laid down upon the bed, and I am sure you are ill enough.'

We are prepared to hear Miss Bates's white lie when she returns and to see Emma in the superior position of knowing that it is a lie. Instead Miss Bates says:

'You will excuse her not coming to you – she is not able – she is gone into her own room – I want her to lie down upon the bed. "My dear," said I, "I shall say you are laid down upon the bed:" but, however, she is not; she is walking about the room.'

Again, the figure of fun has rather turned the tables on us.

That episode comes immediately after Emma's much more serious lapse in permitting herself a hurtful jibe at Miss Bates during the Box Hill party. Like us, she has let herself be trapped into regarding Miss Bates simply as a figure of fun, something to caricature, and now in her wounded feelings we are reminded that Miss Bates is after all a person. Because she has been treated in the spirit of caricature it is not easy for her serious reaction to be conveyed in her ordinary mode of speech; it is given in what amounts to an aside to Mr Knightley. And it is through its effect on him, one of the full characters, that the reality of her hurt is reinforced. His later reproaches and their sobering effect on Emma bring out the seriousness of the episode. It is taken as the occasion for a short but pregnant discussion of the problems of ridicule. He emphasizes Miss Bates's good points:

> 'Oh!' cried Emma, 'I know there is not a better creature in the world: but you must allow, that what is good and what is ridiculous are most unfortunately blended in her.' 'They are blended,' said he, 'I acknowledge; and, were she prosperous, I could allow much for the occasional prevalence of the ridiculous over the good. Were she a woman of fortune, I would leave every harmless absurdity to take its chance, I would not quarrel with you for any liberties of manner. Were she your equal in situation – but, Emma, consider how far this is from being the case. She is poor; she has sunk from the comforts she was born to; and, if she live to old age, must probably sink more. Her situation should secure your compassion. It was badly done, indeed! – You, whom she had known from an infant, whom she had seen grow up from a period when her notice was an honour, to have you now, in thoughtless spirits, and the pride of the moment, laugh at her, humble her – and before her niece, too – and before others, many of whom (certainly *some*), would be entirely guided by *your* treatment of her.'

He supposed her angry with him, but:

> He had misinterpreted the feelings which had kept her face averted, and her tongue motionless. They were

combined only of anger against herself, mortification, and deep concern ... Never had she felt so agitated, mortified, grieved, at any circumstance in her life. She was most forcibly struck. The truth of his representation there was no denying. She felt it at her heart. How could she have been so brutal, so cruel to Miss Bates!

Although in part her distress is at losing Mr Knightley's good opinion, it still comes mainly from what she sees she has done to Miss Bates; and this represents an intensive irruption of human relevance in a figure we had been invited to think of as far out caricature. It brings up the whole problem of ridicule, which it is easy to believe may have been a real one for Jane Austen. The Letters give evidence enough of an eye for the ridiculous and a witty tongue. But she also had her religious upbringing and serious Christian principles, and the third of the surviving Prayers she wrote includes the passage:

Incline us oh God! to think humbly of ourselves, to be severe only in the examination of our own conduct, to consider our fellow-creatures with kindness, and to judge of all they say and do with that charity which we would desire from them ourselves.

This is the sort of prayer Emma might have uttered after her behaviour to Miss Bates. The device of giving these occasional glimpses of something behind the surface she caricatures is an aspect of the serious moral framework within which Jane Austen wrote; it provides a means of reminding herself and us of the limited validity of ridicule.

CHAPTER 6

Mansfield Park

It naturally happens that when a great writer's best work has been given exhaustive attention critical interest turns with curiosity, and in search of new pastures, to parts of his work that have not conventionally been so highly valued, with the result, for a time at least, of a disproportionately full discussion, sometimes a development of eccentric interpretations, and often exaggerated claims for what was previously treated as inferior work. Because people usually find Fanny Price a much less satisfactory heroine than most of Jane Austen's there was for a long time a tendency to underrate *Mansfield Park*. The swing in the other direction has now reached the point of treating it as in some ways the most important of the novels. Tanner, for instance, writes 'if Fanny Price is her least popular heroine, it is arguable that *Mansfield Park* is her most profound novel (indeed, to my mind, it is one of the most profound novels of the nineteenth century)'.[1]

As several people have observed − though not always agreeing on what to make of it − the morality of *Mansfield Park*, morality with an evangelical tinge, is almost avowedly a central concern. Moral issues, in the wider sense, are part of the texture of all Jane Austen's novels, but the moral problems and messages in this novel are more detachable and paraphrasable than they are in the others. We can too easily become aware, as J.I.M. Stewart suggests, of a distinction between the author's intention and her achievement. Although the idea that she said the novel was to be about ordination is based on a misreading of her letter[2] the mistake was plausible because the conflict between Edmund and Mary Crawford about his taking orders (and taking his clerical duties seriously) is a major statement of their difference of moral outlook. The Letters show that although Jane Austen's opinions were divided or fluctuating about evangelicalism she had some sympathy with it. Edmund of course is not presented as an evangelical, but the rather earnest and conscious attention to moral principles which guides both him and Fanny is in line with that habit of mind. The great emphasis placed by Denis Donaghue and Tony Tanner on the seriousness of the moral concern that underlies many of the themes and incidents is fully justified. In spirit, though concentrating on different aspects of the novel, both these critics follow Lionel Trilling with his view of it as an expression of the conflict between the settled and serious standards developed in English country communities and the superficiality and corrupting triviality of metropolitan sophistication.

The moral substance of the book which these accounts draw attention to in their different ways must be given weight in our reading and appreciation of what Jane Austen achieves. But it is equally true that Fanny is offered as the most adequate representative and spokesman of the values the novel endorses, and if she is felt to be an unacceptable heroine something has gone wrong. This strikes me as a dilemma which is not fully recognized by critics who give the novel such high praise. That Jane Austen should have created Fanny Price as a heroine presents a puzzling problem.

It seems reasonably certain that she must have taken the girl's name (whether deliberately or forgetfully) from Crabbe. The last of the Marriages in *The Parish Register* is described in the Argument as 'Attempt to seduce a Village Beauty: Persuasion and Reply: the Event', and it tells of Sir Edward Archer, 'an amorous knight', shunned by maidens chaste and lovely, who tries to win the love of his bailiff's daughter, making her what might ambiguously sound like an offer of eventual marriage. The bailiff's daughter is named Fanny Price. We know how greatly Jane Austen admired Crabbe's work and it seems safe to assume that she would read 'The Parish Register' soon after it appeared among *Poems* of 1807 when she was living in Southampton. By the time she began *Mansfield Park* in 1811 she may have forgotten where the name came from. (This is relatively unremarkable among creative writers: Eliot said that he must have borrowed Madame Sosostris from Aldous Huxley's Madame Sesostris in *Crome Yellow* which he read only a year before writing *The Waste Land*, but he was nevertheless 'unconscious of the borrowing'.[3]) The episode in 'The Parish Register' is not one of Crabbe's more effective tales and might not stay vividly in mind, but there is enough likeness of character and situation between his Fanny Price and the heroine of *Mansfield Park* for the name to carry the right associations. His Fanny Price 'was lovely and was chaste':

> To her the Knight with gentle looks drew near,
> And timid voice assumed, to banish fear

trying to tempt her by vividly contrasting the luxury he could offer with the hardships she would suffer as the wife of a ploughman:

> To this the damsel, meekly firm, replied

in effect that what was good enough for her mother was good enough for her; the Knight thereupon relented and befriended the youth to whom Fanny was pledged.

The differences between Crabbe's rather feeble little episode and the themes of *Mansfield Park* emphasize Jane Austen's closely considered, independent treatment of material that even as good a writer as Crabbe was content to handle along lines of well worn convention. Fanny Price of 'The Parish Register' was meekly willing to follow her mother's pattern of life and to brush aside without a serious thought the forbidding picture painted by Sir Edward, but in the Portsmouth scenes of *Mansfield Park* Jane Austen looked clearsightedly at what a humble marriage might really mean. Again, the character and moral taste of each Fanny Price worked something of a miracle in their suitors, but Sir Edward Archer's briefly announced befriending of his virtuous rival is simple fairy-tale stuff compared with Henry Crawford's clearly examined effort and ultimate failure to change his habits and standards. Sir Edward, expatiating on the delights Fanny can anticipate if she yields to him, tells her:

> Your female friends, though gayest of the gay,
> Shall see you happy, and shall, sighing, say,
> While smother'd envy rises in the breast, –
> 'Oh! that we lived so beauteous and so bless'd!'

Jane Austen exposes her heroine to the same temptation but in the more enticing form given it by a woman, when Mary Crawford exclaims:

> Oh! that I could transport you for a short time into our circle in town, that you might understand how your power over Henry is thought of there! Oh! the envyings and heart-burnings of dozens and dozens! the wonder, the incredulity that will be felt at hearing what you have done!

Jane Austen, it goes without saying, is dealing in an infinitely subtler way with the sort of temptation to which each Fanny is exposed. Her Fanny really would have been married and has no reciprocated pledge of love with another man, a full and complicated context for the problem is created and closely explored, and above all the representative of worldly values is a fully realized individual person, not a conventional puppet, and the background of his values and way of life is brought into convincing existence. But although the cardboard figure of Sir Edward Archer can scarcely be traced at all in Henry Crawford, Jane Austen's Fanny Price still comes too recognizably from the same line of meekly moral heroines as Crabbe's. Their morality is unobjectionable except that it is not particularly theirs; it seems ready-made, quite becoming in style and fit for any young lady of the period. In this quality Fanny differs from all Jane Austen's other heroines, even (I think) from Elinor Dashwood.

In effect the novel comes to an end with the break between the Crawfords and the representatives of the Park. The winding up account which follows is fairly long and Jane Austen could hardly have done without it. But the introductory tense is worth noticing. Fanny, she says, 'must have been' happy in spite of everything. And of Henry Crawford again, 'there would have been' every probability of felicity for him 'could he have been' satisfied with the conquest of one amiable woman's affections. The whole final summary has the manner of looking back at the finished novel and giving an account of what happened afterwards – rather as Jane Austen indulged her family by telling them what happened to Jane Fairfax after her marriage. And though she does arrange for Edmund to fall in love with Fanny so that they can live happily ever after she does it in a deliberately perfunctory and ironic way. The last chapter consists in reflections on the novel and the author's privileged speculations on what happened afterwards.

We might be tempted to see the break with the Crawfords as the final vindication and acceptance of the standards of Mansfield. But the standards of Mansfield as

we actually have them in the substance of the novel are a
very doubtful quantity. Henry Crawford's effort at reform,
after all, is ruined by his affair with Maria, a product of
Mansfield. And the disastrous failure of Sir Thomas in the
upbringing of three out of his four children, a failure
demonstrated in the novel and dwelt on emphatically in
the conclusion, means that the keystone in the moral and
social structure of Mansfield – Sir Thomas himself – to be
very seriously flawed. The extent to which Maria and Julia
are presented as victims of the way of life developed at
Mansfield is not always given serious enough attention.
Maria's loveless marriage was engineered by Mrs Norris in
full accord with the ethos which saw marriage as a move
in the business of economic and social bargaining between
the country families; and it is exactly parallel with the
metropolitan marriage of Mary Crawford's friend Janet
Fraser. The parallel fundamentally modifies any simple
contrast between the metropolitan code and the code of
Mansfield Park. The magnificent scene between Crawford
and Maria at the iron gate and the ha-ha which divide Mr
Rushworth's little wood from his park crystallizes this
aspect of life at Mansfield. It is on the surface a simple
emblematic enactment of Maria's consenting to elope
with Crawford, putting herself beyond the pale and
risking, as Fanny says, tearing her gown and slipping into
the ha-ha, the invisible divide. But it does more than this.
It presents Maria's plight in a way that compels sympathy
in spite of her unappealing ways. She is a fairly intelligent
girl, bright enough to have attracted Crawford, at least for
a flirtation, and she recognizes bitterly the trap she is in.
He refers to her engagement, saying 'You have a very
smiling scene before you.' She replies, '"Do you mean
literally or figuratively? Literally I conclude. Yes, certainly,
the sun shines and the park looks very cheerful. But
unluckily that iron gate, that ha-ha, give me a feeling of

restraint and hardship. I cannot get out, as the starling said." As she spoke, and it was with expression, she walked to the gate; he followed her.'

The enclosing bounds, which appear to Maria like the starling's cage, are not only the boundaries of the little wood but her engagement, and not only her engagement but the social network of respectable and prosperous country families in which Mansfield Park is a nodal point. The elegant and decorous prison is an aspect of the stately home that the two daughters see most clearly. It comes out rather pathetically in the winding up when Julia's elopement with her suitably null young man is explained:

> She had been allowing his attentions some time, but with very little idea of ever accepting him; and, had not her sister's conduct burst forth as it did, and her increased dread of her father and of home, on that event – imagining its certain consequence to herself would be greater severity and restraint – made her hastily resolve on avoiding such immediate horrors at all risks, it is probable that Mr Yates would never have succeeded. She had not eloped with any worse feelings than those of selfish alarm.

Of course Jane Austen registers contempt for a girl like Julia, but there is pity too; she is a victim of the prevailing spirit of Mansfield. It is a spirit that has prevailed through the placid vacuity of Lady Bertram and the failure of Sir Thomas to see through Mrs Norris or to establish any warmth of relationship with his children. This last defect is displayed for us in the scene with Maria when Sir Thomas, realizing what a fool she has got herself engaged to, offers to get her out of it. Jane Austen had already written the scene between Mr Bennet and Elizabeth in a similar situation and shown very movingly an affectionate,

mutually trustful father-daughter relation. Now she shows
the complete absence of those qualities:

> With solemn kindness Sir Thomas addressed her; told
> her his fears, inquired into her wishes, entreated her to
> be open and sincere, and assured her that every incon-
> venience should be braved, and the connection given
> up, if she felt herself unhappy in the prospect of it. He
> would act for her and release her. Maria had a moment's
> struggle as she listened, and only a moment's: when her
> father ceased, she was able to give her answer immedi-
> ately, decidedly, and with no apparent agitation. She
> thanked him for his great attention, his paternal kind-
> ness, but he was quite mistaken in supposing she had
> the smallest desire of breaking through her engagement,
> or was sensible of any change of opinion or inclination
> since her forming it. She had the highest esteem for Mr
> Rushworth's character and disposition, and could not
> have a doubt of her happiness with him.

Maria was of course smarting under Henry Crawford's
failure to carry his flirtation with her any further, and that
confirmed her determination to marry and escape:

> 'He should not have to think of her as pining in the
> retirement of Mansfield for *him*, rejecting Sotherton
> and London, independence and splendour for *his* sake.
> Independence was more needful than ever; the want of
> it at Mansfield more sensibly felt. She was less and less
> able to endure the restraint which her father imposed.
> The liberty which his absence had given was now
> become absolutely necessary.'

If we are tempted to say that Fanny represents the true
spirit of Mansfield and restores the place to itself we should

realize that this is an interpretation for which Jane Austen gives no support. It *may* be that previous generations had produced fewer Marias and Julias and Toms and more Edmunds, fewer Lady Bertrams and Mrs Norrises and more Sir Thomases, but Jane Austen offers nothing on which to base such optimism. Fanny's moral stand has to be made *against* Mansfield. She would have had Sir Thomas's sanction in holding out against the theatricals, but she is deprived even of his support when she resists advantageous marriage to a man whom she doesn't love and whose moral outlook she mistrusts. Certainly she valued Mansfield for its civilized order and decorum, and for the restraint and tranquillity which we are told Maria hated, but in the profounder matters of personal good feeling and insight into the moral worth of other people, she helped to alter Mansfield, to change it from what it has been shown to be all through the novel. The need to do this produces the sharpest conflict in her, since she also loves so much that Mansfield holds for her, and respects so much of Sir Thomas's code.

Mansfield Park is the novel that deals most fully with the conditions necessary for moral development. One condition is the inculcation of a satisfactory moral code and the provision of good personal examples in early life; this condition the Crawfords lacked. In particular, the principle of sacrificing immediate pleasure to duty was crucial. Had Henry Crawford, says Jane Austen;

> done as he intended, and as he knew he ought, by going down to Everingham after his return from Portsmouth, he might have been deciding his own happy destiny. But he was pressed to stay for Mrs Fraser's party; his staying was made of flattering consequence, and he was to meet Mrs Rushworth there. Curiosity and vanity were both engaged, and the temptation of

immediate pleasure was too strong for a mind unused to make any sacrifices to right.

And Maria and Julia, so Sir Thomas decided in reflecting on the mistakes in their education,

> had never been properly taught to govern their inclinations and tempers, by that sense of duty which can alone suffice . . . and of the necessity of self-denial and humility, he feared they had never heard from any lips that could profit them.

But the implication of the story is that training in good principles is not enough: the moral code and the good examples achieve nothing unless there is also good natural quality in the individual. Tom and Edmund, both exposed to the Mansfield training, but differing in personality, grow up into morally different people, Tom spoilt in part by the self-consequence of the eldest son. However, as she shows in *Sense and Sensibility* too, Jane Austen believed that the chastening effects of illness might bring out the better side of a personality. In Tom the happy chance of a nearly fatal illness brought reformation.

> 'He was better for ever for his illness. He had suffered and had learnt to think, two advantages that he had never known before . . . He became what he ought to be, useful to his father, steady and quiet, not living for himself.'

Fanny, needless to say, had had ample opportunity for suffering and the practice of self-denial and humility. But this alone would not have been enough, and if we consider the Price family we can see clearly Jane Austen's assumption that people, even members of the same family, differ in their natural qualities. 'The first solid consolation which Fanny received for the evils of home' on her return to Portsmouth was her coming to realize the natural good qualities of Susan in spite of 'the determined character of her general manners':

> 'Susan saw that much was wrong at home, and wanted to set it right. That a girl of fourteen, acting only on her own unassisted reason, should err in the method of reform was not wonderful; and Fanny soon became more disposed to admire the natural light of the mind which could so early distinguish justly, than to censure severely the fault of conduct to which it led. Susan was only acting on the same truths, and pursuing the same system, which her own judgment acknowledged, but which her more supine and yielding temper would have shrunk from asserting. Susan tried to be useful, where *she* could only have gone away and cried'

And when Fanny has won Susan's affection and begun to give her some guidance Jane Austen reiterates the conviction of some natural good quality having been at work:

> Her greatest wonder on the subject soon became – not that Susan should have been provoked into disrespect and impatience against her better knowledge – but that so much better knowledge, so many good notions, should have been hers at all; and that, brought up in the midst of negligence and error, she should have formed such proper opinions of what ought to be – she, who had no cousin Edmund to direct her thoughts or fix her principles.

Still a third requirement for moral development, beyond good training and good natural quality, is hinted at: a certain warmth and trustfulness of disposition that allows genuine contact between people. In the regretful reflections that are given to Sir Thomas at the end, he is made to see that one of his errors in the upbringing of his daughters was his own manner which induced their guarded attitude towards him. He laments:

> the totally opposite treatment which Maria and Julia had been always receiving at home, where the excessive indulgence and flattery of their aunt had been continually contrasted with his own severity. He saw how ill he had judged, in expecting to counteract what was wrong in Mrs Norris, by its reverse in himself, clearly saw that he had but increased the evil, by teaching them to repress their spirits in his presence, as to make their real disposition unknown to him.

The same point is made in the early account of Mrs Norris's flattery of them:

> 'it is not very wonderful that with all their promising talents and early information, they should be entirely deficient in the less common acquirements of self-knowledge, generosity, and humility. In every thing but disposition, they were admirably taught. Sir Thomas did not know what was wanting, because, though a truly anxious father, he was not outwardly affectionate, and the reserve of his manner repressed all the flow of their spirits before him.'

The warmth of feeling and the openly affectionate manner that he so lacks are among the qualities that the Crawfords bring to Mansfield, qualities no less important in the development of the story than their liveliness and sophistication. We go badly astray if we think of them *simply* as representatives of the trivial metropolitan code.

Mary Crawford has a cynical kind of smart realism ('I look upon the Frasers to be about as unhappy as most other married people.') and we are certainly not expected to excuse her attitude to Edmund's vocation or her callously frank calculations when his elder brother's illness looks like being fatal. In all this she has the example of the aunt who brought her up, she on whose advice Janet Fraser had relied in accepting Mr Fraser for his wealth. But Mary has natural warmth of heart and decency of feeling in personal relations. Jane Austen is careful to bring this out beyond question, even though she also insists on the mixture of motive behind Mary's kindness, for instance on the occasion of Mrs Norris's angry and insulting reproaches when Fanny declines to take part in the theatricals:

> Edmund was too angry to speak; but Miss Crawford looking for a moment with astonished eyes at Mrs Norris, and then at Fanny, whose tears were beginning to show themselves, immediately said with some keenness, "I do not like my situation; this *place* is too hot for me" – and moved away her chair to the opposite side of the table close to Fanny, saying to her in a kind low whisper as she placed herself, "Never mind, my dear Miss Price – this is a cross evening, – everybody is cross and teasing – but do not let us mind them;" and with pointed attention continued to talk to her and endeavour to raise her spirits, in spite of being out of spirits herself. – By a look at her brother, she prevented any farther entreaty from the theatrical board, and the really good feelings by which she was almost purely governed, were rapidly restoring her to all the little she had lost in Edmund's favour.

Henry Crawford too has this capacity for a genuine flow of feeling towards other people. He is admittedly an irresponsible philanderer but his flirtations with Maria and Julia are a social pastime played with girls who are at least equally selfish and rather more designing. We can assume that he would not have raised a finger to help William Price but for the hope of finding a way to Fanny's affection, and yet when he has secured the boy's promotion and comes to tell of it there is convincing warmth in the way he enters into Fanny's feelings: '"I will not talk of my own happiness," said he, "great as it is, for I think only of yours. Compared with you, who has a right to be happy? I have almost grudged myself my own prior knowledge of what you ought to have known before all the world. I have not lost a moment, however."' And above all the scenes in Portsmouth are designed to show his genuine good feeling and tact in dealing with the embarrassing situation of Fanny in the midst of her dreadful family. However improbable his falling in love with her may remain, the good qualities that make his possible reform not quite inconceivable are conveyed convincingly.

He and his sister are both shown as having elements of moral taste that set them apart from their cheap London companions, the Mrs Frasers and Lady Stornaways. Mary welcomes his determination to marry Fanny and insists that in London he must have a house of his own:

> no longer with the Admiral. My dearest Henry, the advantage to you of getting away from the Admiral before your manners are hurt by the contagion of his, before you have contracted any of his foolish opinions, or learned to sit over your dinner, as if it were the best blessing of life! – *You* are not sensible of the gain, for your regard for him has blinded you; but, in my estimation, your marrying early may be the saving of you. To have seen you grow like the Admiral in word or deed, look or gesture, would have broken my heart.

And in her difficult task of making Crawford falling in love with Fanny seem credible, Jane Austen begins with his appreciation of the frank affection between Fanny and her brother.

> An affection so amiable was advancing each in the opinion of all who had hearts to value any thing good. Henry Crawford was as much struck with it as any. He honoured the warm hearted, blunt fondness of the young sailor . . . and saw, with lively admiration, the glow of Fanny's cheek, the brightness of her eye, the deep interest, the absorbed attention, while her brother was describing any of the imminent hazards, or terrific scenes, which such a period, at sea, must supply.
>
> It was a picture which Henry Crawford had moral taste enough to value. Fanny's attractions increased – increased two-fold – for the sensibility which beautified her complexion and illumined her countenance, was an attraction in itself. He was no longer in doubt of the capabilities of her heart. She had feeling, genuine feeling. It would be something to be loved by such a girl, to excite the first ardours of her young, unsophisticated mind! She interested him more than he had foreseen. A fortnight was not enough. His stay became indefinite.

Jane Austen was evidently aiming – and I think she succeeded – at making the Crawfords genuinely likeable people, though so wrong in their code of conduct, deserving to be liked for good qualities of human feeling that they really possessed and that went much deeper than superficial charm and good manners. What they have is totally unlike the good surface and the calculated manner of good feeling that she studied in Mr William Elliot in *Persuasion*. The Crawfords in fact have certain of the ingredients of civilized morality that most of the inhabitants of Mansfield lack, the warmth of personal response to those around them, the affectionate openness with each other, the indignant perception of the way Fanny is put upon and slighted, qualities that are notably absent in the whole Mansfield family except Edmund. Besides their liveliness they bring to the Mansfield scene a friendly responsiveness to good feelings in others which is a part of 'moral taste'. They are shown as being perceptive of the feelings and the failings and the qualities of the family in a way that Sir Thomas notably isn't.

The more you look at it the more difficult it is to sustain the new theory that Park weighs wholly against London in the moral scales. Maria pulls down Henry morally or pulls him back to what he has been – if he really has been: he would not have to come to the Grant's as a known adulterer. Adultery and open disregard of it is certainly condemned more at Mansfield (and Maria *is* banished), but the natural *basis* of morality in good feeling for others, consideration, the generosity and warmth that makes for trust in personal relationships and allow effective mutual help in moral and personal problems (what Sir Thomas failed in with Maria), in all this substratum of morality the Crawfords are better than the Park as a whole.

It is among the individuals of the story that the various factors making for good morality are distributed – inborn personal quality, sound education in moral principles, good examples, self-discipline acquired through early training in putting duty before pleasure (or through the sobering effects of suffering), and a warmth of contact with other people based on genuine consideration for their feelings. This is an interesting and fruitful way of embodying the theme of moral development in vividly concrete situations and convincingly realized personae.

And yet, and fatally, we are left with Edmund and Fanny, above all Fanny, as the achieved ideal. And Fanny is a dreary, debilitated, priggish goody-goody. I take this to be a central failure in a potentially very fine novel. The problem its presents – why Jane Austen created this heroine – may be impossible to solve but it ought to be focused and recognized for the problem it is.

Naturally, for the special purposes of this novel, Jane Austen wanted someone very different from Elizabeth Bennet; liveliness could be allotted to Mary Crawford. But the other heroines are morally serious without having the unfortunately static perfection of Fanny; Elinor Dashwood comes nearest to being always in the right but her vigour and resilience, especially in her relations with Lucy Steele, give her an entirely different quality from Fanny. Nor do the conception and structure of the novel necessitate such a heroine; Fanny could, for instance, have been allowed to feel a little conflict between Edmund, all good principle and blindness to her devotion, and Henry Crawford with his flattering attentiveness and sensitive adjustment of manner to her feelings. Nor need she have been, for the essential action of the novel, quite so crushed and timid. Jane Austen in fact says as much when she speaks of Susan, the sister from Portsmouth who takes Fanny's place as Lady Bertram's companion at Mansfield: 'Her more fearless disposition and happier nerves made every thing easy to her there. – With quickness in understanding the tempers of those she had to deal with, and no natural timidity to restrain any consequent wishes, she was soon welcome, and useful to all.' *We* might argue that Susan's great advantages lay in being fourteen instead of nine and in having no Mrs Norris to contend with, but this is not what Jane Austen chose to say; she chose to attribute the difference to the natural endowments of the two sisters. In other words, she had very definitely wanted this timid and crushed heroine. She might, of course, have written the kind of novel in which a timid girl of nine brought into the dreadful Mansfield family was shown as inevitably growing up to be a drip; but in fact Fanny is offered as the ideal, the ideal wife for Edmund, the ideal daughter for Sir Thomas. Or again, being subtler and more modern, we could imagine Fanny being ostensibly presented as all pious perfection but obliquely shown to be a sly little creep who manages to put everyone else in the wrong and turns out to be a cuckoo in the nest. But that, I feel sure, would be to make the kind of tortuous blunder that Edmund Wilson made over *The Turn of the Screw*. We have to accept it that Jane Austen found Fanny appealing and offered her as a satisfactory heroine.

She does, it is true, allow her one moment of failure, a moment deliberately engineered by Jane Austen. At the end of Volume I, the first big climax when Sir Thomas unexpectedly returns from the West Indies, Fanny has just yielded under pressure, against all her principles, to take a small part in the full rehearsal of the play. This does heighten the impact of the sudden return – it means that Fanny is saved by the bell – but it also breaks the pattern of her heroic adherence to sound principle in face of social pressure. It may represent the realistic novelist in Jane Austen recognizing the probabilities in such a situation, but it seems a departure from all that we have been asked to accept in the way of quietly determined resolution in the heroine, and this one intrusion of natural weakness disturbs the pattern of successful singlehanded resistance to the theatricals (which are important of course as a serious misjudgment on the borderline of morals and manners). In fact Jane Austen seems to feel a need to restore the pattern, and it looks perhaps as though we too are meant to accept the account Edmund gives his father of Fanny's part in the whole affair. Though perhaps not literally untrue it still manages to conceal her final lapse and convey a false impression:

'We have all been more or less to blame,' said he, 'every one of us, excepting Fanny. Fanny is the only one who had judged rightly throughout, who has been consistent. *Her* feelings have been steadily against it from first to last. She never ceased to think of what was due to you. You will find Fanny every thing you could wish.'

If we accept the impression Sir Thomas would receive from this we are given once more the faultless and morally indomitable heroine.

There are several possible and partial explanations of Jane Austen's creating such a character. *Mansfield Park* was the first novel of hers to be conceived from the start as something for the general reading public. *Susan, Sense and Sensibility* and *Pride and Prejudice* had all been based on work in which the amusement of her family had been a big part of the original intention. With *Mansfield Park* she had the responsibility of a serious novelist writing for the public. This could have led her towards a more serious theme, though it need not have produced such a heroine. The Letters show that she was at times, though rather against her inclination, impressed with the evangelical current in the Church, and although Edmund is not an evangelical he and Fanny share many of the attitudes which that current of thought was introducing even among more conventional churchmen. And there was evidently a welcoming audience for someone like Fanny, to judge by the success of the novel. The distressed and perfectly virtuous heroine looks back to Pamela and forward to some of the Victorian characters; and in fact reality almost caught up with it in the person of Jenny Lind, the nineteenth century singer, who is interesting in this context not only because she had unsatisfactory parents and left her home in adolescence but because her dislike of the theatre led her at 28 to give up singing in opera altogether. At about this time she was engaged to a young Indian army officer, but he and his mother had such strict evangelical principles that they 'insisted that Jenny Lind should cut herself off from the stage by an official statement to that effect in the marriage agreement. The mother detested the very thought of actors and actresses.' Although Jenny Lind herself found the conditions of theatrical life intolerable she objected to this, as well as to her fiancé's insistence that he should have control of her earnings, a part of which she had always contributed to charity. She broke off the engagement.[4] And of course Jenny Lind suffered a good deal from the vague ill health for which people at that time were sent to the European spas. There was undoubtedly a strong current of feeling in favour of this feminine ideal, a current flowing from the eighteenth through the nineteenth century, and Fanny Price could easily find a welcome. But Jane Austen never created such a character again, and it seems unlikely that the receptiveness of the reading public is enough to account for it.

Possibly we have to turn to elements of Jane Austen's personal experience as contributory factors making for her interest in such a character. Fanny is very much a Cinderella. Jane Austen had gone through the uncomfortable years of restricted income after her father's death, with no proper home of her own; and even in 1811 when she began *Mansfield Park* she was still the poor relation living with her mother and sister in the very small cottage that her rich brother had made available. She was also the younger sister; we can too easily forget how much in the background she was for most of her life compared with Cassandra. Chapman makes the point usefully: 'There was a doctrine in the family, which Jane steadily supported, if she did not start it, that in all important respects the elder sister was the superior. This view was not many years ago found to persist in a branch of the family, the ladies of which made it plain that Cassandra and her drawing were not less interesting in their eyes than Jane and her writing.'[5] Jane Austen was working on *Mansfield Park* when *Sense and Sensibility* had been accepted and was just coming out and there was therefore some slight chance of her talent being recognized. In these circumstances it may be that a Cinderella figure had a great appeal for her. To fill that role a girl must be very good, must be despised and ill-used, must endure it patiently, and must seem quite unattractive until some turn of fortune leads to her real quality being discerned. In *Mansfield Park* she saw no way of combining those requirements with anything more attractive. It was not until Anne Elliot in *Persuasion* that she solved that problem, and then by a profoundly different view of the whole situation.

This appeal of the Cinderella figure, the evangelical trend of the time, and a receptive reading public, may be parts of the explanation, but I still feel that the problem is far from solved. I am sure that it really is a problem. Less than four years after *Mansfield Park* was finished Fanny Knight, her favourite niece, was persuading her current young man to read some of Jane Austen's novels and wickedly luring him to comment on them without revealing that her favourite aunt had written them. Fanny Knight passed on the comments, which evidently included objections to the imperfections of some of the heroines. After upbraiding her for the shameless trick and telling her to confess and apologise to him, Jane Austen adds 'He and I should not in the least agree of course, in our ideas of Novels and Heroines; – pictures of perfection as you know make me sick and wicked' (23 March 1817). The puzzle is that this, which is so authentically the voice of Jane Austen, was written by the creator of Fanny Price.

CHAPTER 7

Northanger Abbey

Under its original title of *Susan*, *Northanger Abbey* was the first of her novels to be accepted for publication, by Crosby in 1803; it was advertised but never appeared, a disappointment for her during the period in which she did relatively little literary work. In October 1808 her brother's offer of Chawton Cottage meant the possibility of a new beginning with a home of their own for the two sisters and their mother. It was now that Jane Austen decided so seriously on a further attempt at publication that she began to put aside from her very small income a reserve of money to meet the loss she expected to incur in getting a publisher to bring out a book at her own expense. But first she tried to get Crosby to bring out *Susan*. He refused, though he also insisted on retaining his rights in it (since he had bought it for ten pounds) and declined to let her try another publisher unless she bought back the manuscript for ten pounds. She left it with him, and two years later, after the move to Chawton, she had arranged for Egerton to publish *Sense and Sensibility*. Then came *Pride and Prejudice*, *Mansfield Park* and *Emma*. From late in 1815 until August 1816 she was writing *Persuasion*, but during that period her brother bought back the manuscript of *Susan* for her and some time in 1816 she put it into a form that she thought would do for publication. The heroine's name was changed to Catherine but there is no external evidence about the extent of the revisions she made.

However, it seems extremely probable that enough revision had been going on in 1816 for Jane Austen or her sister to refer to it in letters. Early in 1817 when the seriousness of her illness was known her niece Fanny Knight was writing rather frequently and in one of her letters must have asked about the progress of her aunt's writing. From Jane Austen's reply it is evident that Fanny knew about the revised book, since it was possible to refer to Catherine without explanation, and to imply that Fanny knew how long it was. Writing on 13 March 1817 Jane Austen said 'I *will* answer your kind questions more than you expect. Miss Catherine is put upon the Shelve for the present, and I do not know that she will ever come out; – but I have something ready for Publication, which may appear about a twelvemonth hence. It is short, about the length of Catherine.' The finished work, of course, was *Persuasion* and the two were brought out posthumously in four volumes, with Catherine entitled *Northanger Abbey*.

The significant points in this history are:

1. *Northanger Abbey* was a transition between the early work written largely with a view to family entertainment and the later more professionally conceived writing for the public (in this way falling into the same category as *Sense and Sensibility* and *Pride and Prejudice*).
2. With the crucial decision to start again on a serious attempt at publishing her work she turned first to *Northanger Abbey* and would have been willing for it to appear in its original 1803 version.
3. At the height of her mature powers, after *Emma*, she recovered it at her own expense and again prepared it for publication.
4. In the following year, towards the end of her life, she was still contemplating publication but had doubts about it.

Thus very interestingly *Northanger Abbey* brings together her early life as a writer and the end of it when, although she was physically ill, her literary judgment was alert and sensitive, as the revision of the last chapters of *Persuasion* testifies. Between 1803, when she would have liked to publish *Susan*, and 1817, when she was doubtful about publishing it even after revision, the standards by which she judged her own work had very much changed.

The history of the book challenges us to achieve something of her own view of it and try to see what it possesses that appealed to her at the time of her full development as well as what the weaknesses were that made her hesitate. The age and naivety of the heroine might tempt us to suppose that this is a novel specially suited for young and inexperienced readers – I believe it is sometimes prescribed for school reading – when it can more appropriately be seen as a difficult book demanding the discriminations of a practised reader.

As most critics have felt, the burlesque of the Gothic is too heavy-handed. It is the kind of work that could easily arise out of the joking exaggeration meant for family entertainment, where a younger member of the family is amusing parents and older siblings and the exaggeration amounts to a disavowal of serious pretensions. Such things as the old laundry lists discovered in the cabinet instead of the manuscript Henry Tilney jokingly forecasts that begins 'Oh! thou – whomsoever thou mayst be, into whose hands these memoirs of the wretched Matilda may fall' (p. 160) are very much school magazine humour. There is a theory, offered by C.S. Emden (*Notes and Queries*, CXCV (1950) 407–10), that the Gothic episodes were a later addition to an early book which burlesqued only the sentimental novel; the latter, Mr Emden suggests, was written about 1794 and the Gothic burlesque added about 1798. The evidence is very scanty and to me not convincing; in any case, even if this were a correct speculation, it refers to a book completed by 1803 and has no bearing on the question of what Jane Austen thought was worth salvaging in 1816.

For criticism it is more important to notice why the Gothic element seems the least satisfactory part of the novel. There are at least two reasons. One is that a rather slight, rather superficial development is involved in Catherine's recovery from these delusions, compared with the important psychological advance implied by her disillusioned appraisal of Isabella Thorpe. Discarding the Gothic nonsense allows her to emerge from a particular form of childish makebelieve and see the superficial features of life with General Tilney in a less distorted fashion, but it leaves her still a child in her judgment of his character; though she gives up the notion that he poisoned his wife she remains a credulous child in supposing that he really meant what he said, for instance about the unimportance of money to him compared with his children's happiness. Compared with this, seeing through Isabella Thorpe is a step towards becoming a grown-up. The first revision of her attitude to Isabella follows the news that James Morland has been jilted for Captain Tilney, and with Henry Tilney's help Catherine examines her state of mind and decides that the break with Isabella is for her not quite so afflicting as she would have expected. The decisive disillusionment occurs when she gets Isabella's letter entreating her to help in getting James back after Captain Tilney's flirtation has ended: 'She must think me an idiot, or she could not have written so; but perhaps this has served to make her character better known to me than mine is to her. I see what she has been about. She is a vain coquette, and her tricks have not answered. I do not believe she had ever any regard either for James or for me, and I wish I had never known her'.

The relative unimportance of the Gothic part of the heroine's development is one thing that reduces its value and leaves it superficial. The other objection is that it creates too great a tension in our conception of Catherine; it stretches her naivety too far in the direction of sheer silliness. The rather implausibly exaggerated element of caricature here is not effectively enough fused with the natural portraiture needed for her to be the heroine. This is the same difficulty that Jane Austen met in handling Marianne Dashwood's wild romanticism; that was treated in the spirit of caricature, as are Catherine's Gothic fancies, but some sense of dislocation occurs when we have to take very seriously the miseries of Marianne's broken heart. The difficulty is felt less with Catherine, because the emotional pitch is lower, but the problem of handling the one figure partly as caricature and partly as credible portrait has not been solved.

Catherine is one of the heroines whose greatest interest for Jane Austen lies in her development, development towards better sense and sounder judgment, in a girl who, however attractive, has faults or inadequacies. Emma's self-discovery is the supremely successful example; the change in Marianne comes about too abruptly and melo-dramatically after her illness. Catherine falls between the two in the success with which her development is shown. Like Emma on Box Hill, Catherine is taught her most striking lesson by her lover – when Henry Tilney elicits her absurd suspicions about his father. This degree of active relationship between the girl and her lover contrib-utes to making a more convincing union between Emma and Mr Knightley, and between Catherine and Henry Tilney than the merely postulated marriage of Marianne and Colonel Brandon.

Of course one can easily make a mechanical application of Freudian ideas (as I believe Geoffrey Gorer has done) and say that these girls whose older lovers help to guide them as they grow up are in psychological effect marrying their fathers. It illuminates nothing to say this. To import psychoanalytic ideas when there is no problem for them to solve is futile. There is nothing puzzling or inexplicable at the conscious level about any of these marriages given the conditions of the period. Age disparity between husband and wife was common, and as the man would usually have educational advantages beyond the girl, as well as more experience, there can be nothing strange about a girl's being guided by her lover if she was guidable at all (as wives like Mrs Bennet obviously were not).

The portrait of Catherine is a big part of the book's achievement. Its success lies in the presentation of a girl who combines extreme inexperience with real charm and with the promise of good sense as she gains experience. Jane Austen describes her explicitly, but indirectly, by making Eleanor apply to Catherine the ironic description of Isabella Thorpe that Henry offers when it seems that Frederick Tilney is going to marry her:

> 'It is all over with Frederick indeed! He is a deceased man – defunct in understanding. Prepare for your sister-in-law, Eleanor, and such a sister-in-law as you must delight in! – Open, candid, artless, guileless, with affections strong but simple, forming no pretensions, and knowing no disguise.'
> 'Such a sister-in-law, Henry, I should delight in,' said Eleanor, with a smile.

That very compact piece of dialogue suggests mature skill, combining as it does the ironic description of Isabella, the summary of Catherine's character without the direct intervention of the author, and Eleanor's approval of Catherine as a bride for Henry.

Catherine is conceived of as having much more solid sense and decisiveness and much more power of indepen-

dently learning from experience than, for instance, Harriet
Smith, whose charming naivety is of the conventional
kind that Mr Elton can condescendingly appreciate. Catherine is shown as being no *more* taken in by false charm
and sophistication than her elder brother; and one of the
simpler ironies of the story is provided by James's recommendation to her to take advantage of the inestimable
good fortune of companionship with Isabella Thorpe; it is
with his encouragement that her intimacy with Isabella is
confirmed and extended. And in the upshot, when his
engagement is broken, James is given a more naive
reaction even than Catherine's, since he is made to
contrast Isabella's duplicity with the honest heart of her
brother, whom Catherine saw through long ago:

> Poor Thorpe is in town: I dread the sight of him; his
> honest heart would feel so much . . . I cannot under-
> stand even now what she would be at, for there could
> be no need of my being played off to make her secure
> of Tilney. We parted at last by mutual consent – happy
> for me had we never met! I can never expect to know
> such another woman!

Jane Austen had no intention of making Catherine the
only naive member of her family.

Catherine's development is only partially due to Henry
Tilney. In fact some of what she owes to him is the subject
of Jane Austen's mockery, notably the lesson on the
picturesque, where what she absorbs is parallel (though at
a higher level of educated taste) to the knowledge of
Gothic novels that she absorbs from Isabella:

> He talked of fore-grounds, distances, and second
> distances – side-screens and perspectives – lights and
> shades; – and Catherine was so hopeful a scholar, that
> when they gained the top of Beechen Cliff, she volun-

tarily rejected the whole city of Bath, as unworthy to make part of a landscape. Delighted with her progress, and fearful of wearying her with too much wisdom at once, Henry suffered the subject to decline.

The picture is of very pleasant young people finding their way about the conventionally cultivated tastes of their time, but also much more seriously engaged in exploring personal relationships and the values they express. The main part of Catherine's development comes as a result of extended experience in a girl of sound principles who has courage and an unaffected openness to experience. For once Jane Austen provided her heroine with more or less adequate parents, matter-of-fact and unimaginative, who kept well in the background but still seen as the source of good principles and good sense. Catherine's openness to her experience, without any self-consciousness or self-congratulation about learning from it, is presented deftly and attractively in the dialogue with Henry after Isabella's jilting of James is known; his helpful, bantering irony is met by her honest directness in discovering her real feelings, and this then wins his genuine admiration and serious compliment:

> 'You feel, I suppose, that, in losing Isabella, you lose half yourself: you feel a void in your heart which nothing else can occupy. Society is becoming irksome; and as for the amusements in which you were wont to share at Bath, the very idea of them without her is abhorrent. You would not, for instance, now go to a ball for the world. You feel that you have no longer any friend to whom you can speak with unreserve; on whose regard you can place dependence; or whose counsel, in any difficulty, you could rely on. You feel all this?'
>
> 'No,' said Catherine, after a few moments' reflection,

'I do not – ought I? To say the truth, though I am hurt and grieved, that I cannot still love her, that I am never to see her again, I do not feel so very, very much afflicted as one would have thought.'

'You feel, as you always do, what is most to the credit of human nature. – Such feelings ought to be investigated, that they may know themselves.'

Her straightforward recognition of having only very moderate feelings registers her recovery from the attraction of the exaggerated effusiveness of the sentimental novel and of Isabella's conversational technique.

But Catherine would have had no opportunity to develop in the direction of the values that Henry and Eleanor help her to understand if it had not been for the struggle she had during the Bath period to break free from the standards of the Thorpes – which were also her brother's while he was infatuated with Isabella. For all the comedy convention within which the episodes are treated the psychological struggle to defy the demands of her immediate companions is made critical for Catherine's development. First, John Thorpe tricks her into not waiting for the Tilneys to take her for a walk they had arranged. This involves no social struggle for her, but it displays her simple and unaffected determination to apologize to the Tilneys and put things right, the episode ending with the very funny and charming reconciliation with Henry in the theatre:

'But, Mr Tilney, why were *you* less generous than your sister? If she felt such confidence in my good intentions, and could suppose it to be only a mistake, why should *you* be so ready to take offence?'

'Me! – I take offence!'

'Nay, I am sure by your look, when you came into the box, you were angry.'

'I angry! I could have no right.'

'Well, nobody would have thought you had no right who saw your face.'

He replied by asking her to make room for him, and talking of the play.

In this first episode things are put right by her simple openness and the flatteringly obvious way she has fallen for Henry.

But in the incident on the Crescent when the plan for going to Clifton is renewed and Catherine's company demanded by the Thorpes in spite of her engagement to the Tilneys, the struggle is serious. It forms a decisive part of Catherine's growing up. She was guided, one may say, by conventionally sound social principles in not breaking an undertaking and not being uncivil to her friends – but because this is a novel and not a treatise the sound principles are complicated by the fact that they support the plan that gives her the company of the entrancing Henry. Isabella is prompt in scoring off that:

> The three others still continued together, walking in a most uncomfortable manner to poor Catherine; some-times not a word was said, sometimes she was again attacked with supplications or reproaches, and her arm was still linked within Isabella's, though their hearts were at war. At one moment she was softened, at another irritated; always distressed, but always steady.
>
> 'I did no think you had been so obstinate, Catherine.' said James; 'you were not used to be so hard to persuade; you once were the kindest, best-tempered of my sisters.'
>
> 'I hope I am not less so now,' she replied, very feelingly; 'but indeed I cannot go. If I am wrong, I am doing what I believe to be right.'
>
> 'I suspect,' said Isabella, in a low voice, 'there is no great struggle.'

Thorpe then comes back from his insolent mission of telling the Tilneys that Catherine has recollected a prior engagement – and this of course adds lying to rudeness. Catherine not only shakes the others off physically ('Let me go, Mr Thorpe; Isabella, do not hold me') but she shakes off some of her naive trust in other people by realizing that John Thorpe is thoroughly untrustworthy:

'Mr Thorpe had no business to invent such a message. If I had thought it right to put it off, I could have spoken to Miss Tilney myself. This is only doing it in a ruder way; and how do I know that Mr Thorpe has – he may be mistaken again perhaps; he led me into one act of rudeness by his mistake on Friday.'

The seriousness of Catherine's decision as a matter of principle is reinforced by the rather improbably careful reflections she is given as she hurries away to catch up with the Tilneys:

Away walked Catherine in great agitation, as fast as the crowd would permit her, fearful of being pursued, yet determined to persevere. As she walked, she reflected on what had passed. It was painful to her to disappoint and displease them, particularly to displease her brother; but she could not repent her resistance. Setting her own inclination apart, to have failed a second time in her engagement to Miss Tilney, to have retracted a promise voluntarily made only five minutes before, and on a false pretence too, must have been wrong. She had not been withstanding them on selfish principles alone, she had not consulted merely her own gratification; *that* might have been ensured in some degree by the excursion itself, by seeing Blaize Castle; no, she had attended to what was due to others, and to her own character in their opinion.

That forms a serious pendant to the dramatic struggle on the Crescent, and then the episode ends in the comedy of her agitated apologies when she bursts in on the surprised Tilneys.

It makes a turning point, because it introduces the General's plot to get the supposed heiress for his younger son. And it transfers Catherine from the milieu of the Thorpes to the milieu of the Tilneys, a fundamental change reflected in the physical change from life at Bath to life at the Abbey. The essential point is that the transfer depended on her own courage, her defiance of close companions, including her elder brother.

The struggle on the Crescent puts Catherine into the more highly civilized world represented by Henry and Eleanor. It is important to notice the sureness of Jane Austen's discrimination here. Catherine's success is not that of getting into a higher social class than the shabbily pretentious middle-class world of the Thorpes. As in *Mansfield Park*, the more civilized standards at the Abbey are not represented by the place and the family as a whole. The moral taste, social consideration, good principle, appreciation of sincerity and good feeling in others, these things are found only in Henry and Eleanor, not in the Tilneys as a family.

The other two, the General and Captain Frederick, for all their wealth and social advantages, are shown as belonging inescapably to the same world as the Thorpes – Captain Tilney in the vulgarity and triviality of his flirtation which makes him a fitting associate for Isabella; the General in the mercenary scheming by which he becomes the dupe of Thorpe's greedy imagination while he imagines he is outsmarting Thorpe by getting Catherine for Henry. The General and his elder son are spiritually united with the Thorpes, however far above them in social consequence. Catherine has achieved a psychological rather than a social promotion.

The division of the Tilney family, two with moral taste and two without, is handled subtly and maturely. Both filial duty and good manners keep Eleanor and Henry from any open expression of the schism. Henry evades a direct answer to Catherine's naive wonder about Captain Tilney's intentions in flirting with Isabella when he knew her to be engaged. And the conflict Eleanor feels comes virtually to open expression in her distress at having to convey to Catherine the General's order of expulsion; when Catherine asks 'Have I offended the General?' she replies 'Alas! for my feelings as a daughter, all that I know, all that I answer for is, that you can have given him no just cause of offence'.

Eleanor and Henry can, in this family situation, only have an unspoken alliance of ironic detachment. If the handling of this alliance was in the original version of the novel Jane Austen must very early have had a remarkably sure and delicate touch. They have not only to avoid any breach of deference to their father and any open condemnation of members of their family, which would be embarrassing to a guest, but they must at the same time indicate clearly their knowledge of their father's character defects and express their own detachment from his scale of values.

When Catherine is astonished that Henry is not taking literally his father's assurances that whatever there is in the house will be enough for dinner when they visit the parsonage at Woodston he quietly avoids a direct reply:

> 'But how can you think of such a thing, after what the General said? when he particularly desired you not to give yourself any trouble, because *any thing* would do.'
> Henry only smiled. 'I am sure it is quite unnecessary upon your sister's account and mine. You must know it to be so; and the General made such a point of your

providing nothing extraordinary: – besides, if he had
not said half so much as he did, he has always such an
excellent dinner at home, that sitting down to a
middling one for one day could not signify.'

'I wish I could reason like you, for his sake and my
own. Good bye. As tomorrow is Sunday, Eleanor, I
shall not return.'

'for his sake and my own' is deft and unlaboured. Again,
when Captain Tilney's supposed engagement to Isabella is
being discussed Eleanor asks Catherine about Isabella's
'connexions and fortune':

'Her mother is a very good sort of woman,' was
Catherine's answer.
'What was her father?'
'A lawyer, I believe. – They live at Putney.'
'Are they a wealthy family?'
'No, not very. I do not believe Isabella has any
fortune at all; but that will not signify in your family. –
Your father is so very liberal! He told me the other
day, that he only valued money as it allowed him to
promote the happiness of his children.' The brother and
sister looked at each other. 'But,' said Eleanor, after a
short pause, 'would it be to promote his happiness, to
enable him to marry such a girl? – She must be an
unprincipled one, or she could not have used your
brother so.'

This kind of thing is so dextrous as to suggest mature skill.
It also reflects what must have been a familiar predicament
for Jane Austen, living in the intimate midst of people less
subtle and sensitive than herself, people with whom she
always must live and to whom she was bound by filial and
familial ties which to her represented Christian obligations.
(I am not suggesting, of course, that she had anyone like

General Tilney to put up with – but the same pattern of
conflict and the same need for unspoken disagreement
may easily have been familiar to her.)

A similar success, especially of natural but subtly organized dialogue, is to be found in a very short chapter which
may perhaps have been totally new material inserted
during a late revision. This is Chapter IV of Volume II, or
Chapter 19 of the modern editions. It shows Henry
evading Catherine's forthright inquiries in Bath about his
brother's shortcomings and at the same time leading her a
step towards insight into Isabella and her behaviour with
James and Frederick. Catherine asks Henry to persuade his
brother to go away:

> 'Absence will in time make him comfortable again;
> but he can have no hope here, and it is only staying to
> be miserable.' Henry smiled and said, 'I am sure my
> brother would not wish to do that.'
> 'Then you will persuade him to go away?'
> 'Persuasion is not at command; but pardon me, if I
> cannot even endeavour to persuade him. I have myself
> told him that Miss Thorpe is engaged. He knows what
> he is about, and must be his own master.'
> 'No, he does not know what he is about,' cried
> Catherine; 'he does not know the pain he is giving my
> brother. Not that James ever told me so, but I am sure
> he is very uncomfortable.'
> 'And are you sure it is my brother's doing?'
> 'Yes, very sure.'
> 'Is it my brother's attentions to Miss Thorpe, or Miss
> Thorpe's admission of them, that gives the pain?'
> 'Is not it the same thing?'
> 'I think Mr Morland would acknowledge a differ-
> ence. No man is offended by another man's admiration
> of the woman he loves; it is the woman only who can
> make it a torment.'

Catherine blushed for her friend, and said, 'Isabella is wrong.'

The whole of this chapter is interesting for its skilful management of tone and the practised command of dialogue. The dialogue here and in the discussion of Frederick's supposed engagement to Isabella strikes me as a much later development than any sustained passages of *Sense and Sensibility*. This short Chapter 19 adds nothing to the narrative; the preceding and following chapters could have been juxtaposed without difficulty. Speculatively too we can notice the bit of dialogue about 'persuasion' and remember that Jane Austen had been working on *Persuasion* at about the same time as – to judge by Fanny Knight's letter – she had been doing some work on 'Catherine'. My own guess – for what a guess is worth – is that the dialogue of Catherine, Henry and Eleanor about Captain Tilney in the closing scenes at Bath and the Abbey scenes is a late revision, done at about the same time as *Persuasion*.

Another minor hint of revision, probably of an expansion not quite successfully dovetailed in, is the sameness of the general pattern with which Chapters X and XII of Volume II end (Chapters 25 and 27 of the continuously numbered editions). And there are no doubt many more hints and clues of this kind that could be followed up in literary detective work, including no doubt even statistical analysis of sentence length and structure. Critically the more important thing is to form some idea of what features of the novel as we have it attracted Jane Austen enough for her to have thought seriously of publication and what features led to Miss Catherine being put upon the 'shelve' and hesitated over.

Almost certainly Jane Austen was dissatisfied with the structure. It falls apart into its two halves, Bath and Northanger. They are tied together by the formation of the Henry-Eleanor-Catherine alliance at Bath and its consolidation at the Abbey; but still the disappearance of the Thorpes, the Allens, James Morland and Captain Tilney leaves rather an emptiness in the second half. The letters from James and Isabella only clinch the outcome of the Isabella-James-Captain Tilney triangle which after all was shown, before we left Bath, well on the way to its conclusion. Only James's letter adds something unexpected in its suggestion that Captain Tilney will really marry Isabella and so gives the occasion for Henry and Eleanor to reveal their father's determination that his children shall marry for money or social position. But after these letters James, Frederick and Isabella just drop out and are not even included in a perfunctory winding up such as Jane Austen often provides. *Northanger Abbey* is in this way in sharp contrast to *Emma*, with its compactness, and also to *Mansfield Park* where a big cast of characters is kept effectively in play almost to the last and the loose ends are all carefully if briefly tied off, and we hear what happened to the Crawfords, the Grants, Mrs Norris and Maria, and Julia and Mr Yates.

The best part of the structure, the nearest approach to what can be called structure at all, is given by Catherine's two lines of development, the social development that allies her to Henry and Eleanor instead of Isabella, and the development of commonsense correctives to romantic fantasy. The two are tied together because she had taken over the taste for Gothic fantasy from Isabella, and her relinquishment of it forms a climax in her relations with Henry – he is the exorcist. At the same time this progress in Catherine is linked with the main twist of plot, the twist emphasized by Lionel Trilling: that when we have been tempted to dismiss Catherine's ideas about evil at the Abbey as a complete load of rubbish the tables are turned on us by the General's sudden and socially violent expulsion of her. We are confronted with the fact that startling and highly unpleasant things – psychologically violent things – can happen even in a milieu where wives are not poisoned or shut away in the cells of old monasteries.

It is undoubtedly a considered twist of plot and a deliberate reminder that even when fantasy has been brought under control there are still alarming things to be faced. Jane Austen underlines Catherine's good sense and courage on the night when the General returns in a rage. She is waiting in her bedroom for Eleanor to come back from seeing who can have arrived so late, waiting in the room where some of her silliest Gothic imaginings were set:

> At that moment Catherine thought she heard her step in the gallery, and listened for its continuance; but all was silent. Scarcely, however, had she convicted her fancy of error, when the noise of something moving close to her door made her start; it seemed as if some one was touching the very doorway – and in another moment a slight motion of the lock proved that some hand must be on it. She trembled a little at the idea of any one's approaching so cautiously; but resolving not to be again overcome by trivial appearances of alarm, or misled by a raised imagination, she stepped quietly forward, and opened the door.

The complete recovery from fanciful alarm is emphasized – only to introduce the shock of the real social outrage. The parallel, and the contrast, with her fanciful alarms when she first came to the Abbey is worked out explicitly again when she goes to bed:

> Heavily past the night. Sleep, or repose that deserved the name of sleep, was out of the question. That room, in which her disturbed imagination had tormented her on her first arrival, was again the scene of agitated sprits

and unquiet slumbers. Yet how different now the source of her inquietude from what it had been then – how mournfully superior in reality and substance! Her anxiety had foundation in fact, her fears in probability; and with a mind so occupied in the contemplation of actual and natural evil, the solitude of her situation, the darkness of her chamber, the antiquity of the building were felt and considered without the smallest emotion; and though the wind was high, and often produced strange and sudden noises throughout the house, she heard it all as she lay awake, hour after hour, without curiosity or terror.

(Notice the phrase 'natural and actual evil', one of those unexpectedly strong expressions that Jane Austen can slip in unobtrusively and without, for many readers, disturbing the polite moderation of most of her prose.)

Catherine's development and the irony of her expulsion, although effective, can hardly compensate for the general weakness of structure. And there are even unexplained features of the mere machinery of the plot, specially how it came about that Thorpe, knowing her brother well, could have decided Catherine was an heiress; and whether Eleanor and Henry after so much conversation with her could have been deceived about her wealth and if not how Henry explained his father's wanting him to marry her. By the standards of plot and structure she had already reached there were enough weaknesses in *Northanger Abbey* to make Jane Austen hesitate.

There remains the fact that she was seriously considering it and might have issued it in some form if she had recovered from her illness. She had not relegated it to the juvenilia with *Lady Susan* or abandoned it as she did *The Watsons*. And so we have to judge what features of it she would have been sorry to sacrifice. One almost certainly is the charm of the heroine; the combination of sheer funniness with charm in some of the scenes involving Catherine (for instance, her apologies to the Tilneys in their drawing room and to Henry at the theatre) is something not quite equalled anywhere else in Jane Austen's writing. The development of the heroine, too, is a process that obviously meant a great deal to Jane Austen – to judge by several of the novels – and Catherine's development, especially in its social aspects, has real interest. Isabella Thorpe's vulgarity and self-seeking which link her to Lucy Steele (and really Mrs Elton) are perhaps rather more caricatured than portrayed but still are convincingly dreadful and worth saving, as is the nonentity of Mrs Allen, a precursor of Lady Bertram. And the psychological schism in the Tilney family, with Henry and Eleanor living at a higher standard than their father and brother, is a situation that she uses in variant forms in *Pride and Prejudice*, *Mansfield Park* and *Persuasion* and which evidently seemed significant to her; it still remains a significant source of tension, even in modern families that are much less closely knit and inescapable than those of Jane Austen's period and class. And finally the beautifully judged tone of the dialogue in which the Tilneys' family tensions are revealed – or the guardedness by which Henry and Eleanor prevent the tensions from openly occurring – is something that modern readers and presumably Jane Austen herself would have been sorry to lose.

These possible answers to the question of what in *Northanger Abbey* is successful and what needs excuse as apprentice work may not be right and other readers may make different discriminations. But the question is right and well worth asking, if only because Jane Austen was asking it herself when she possessed standards of judgment based on the achievements of her mature work.

CHAPTER 8

An Introduction to Persuasion

Chawton Cottage is one of the few places of literary pilgrimage that have relevance to an appreciation of the writer who lived there. At some little distance from the great house of the rich brother who provided it, respectable but rather cramped, with the small living room in which Jane Austen wrote – a room shared by her sister Cassandra and her ailing mother and used besides for receiving callers – the house speaks of the close pressure of a social milieu, and heightens our wonder at the work that emerged from it. The older idea that her novels simply offered amusing entertainment for people like those she lived amongst (and their successors down to our own time) has given way to the recognition in her work of a much stronger dislike of the society in which she seemed comfortably embedded, a dislike often implicit, often conveyed in passing and easily ignored, occasionally intense and bitter. In 1940 I published an essay called 'Regulated Hatred: an aspect of Jane Austen'; in 1964 a psychologist colleague who had never heard of that essay mentioned that she had recently tried in vain to recover the pleasure she took in the novels as a girl. 'They used to seem so light and amusing, but they're not like that at all. You know – she *hated* people.' Of course this is too extreme. The urbanity, the charm, the wit and lightness of touch, the good humour, are there as they always were, but the other aspect which readers nowadays notice means that for full enjoyment we have to appreciate a more complex flavour.

The situation of being a poor relation was one that Jane

Austen could share with her sister and their widowed mother. The situation of being the most brilliant, the most sensitive and penetrating member of her family, while she filled the roles of affectionate spinster aunt and of dutiful daughter to a hypochondriac mother, was a situation she could share with no one. It is not surprising, therefore, that variants of the Cinderella story, as well as the psychologically allied story of the foundling princess, should be prominent among the basic themes of her novels.

Anne Elliott, the heroine of *Persuasion*, her last novel, is the most mature and profound of Cinderellas. Earlier, in *Mansfield Park*, she had tried an out-and-out foundling princess and Cinderella in Fanny Price – all moral perfection, thoroughly oppressed, rather ailing, priggish, but finally vindicated and rewarded with the hero – and few people can stomach her. The theme is inevitably difficult to handle. For one thing the fantasy of being mysteriously superior to one's parentage is rather common ('I refused to believe', remarks T.S. Eliot's Lady Elizabeth, 'that my father could have been an ordinary earl! And I couldn't believe that my mother *was* my mother') and commonly unjustified. And the crushed dejection (masking resentment) of the self-cast Cinderellas of real life always provokes a sneaking sympathy for the ugly sisters. The novelist's difficulty with this theme is to secure a lively enough interest in the heroine during the early stages, when the reality of her dejection has to be enforced, and to retain interest and sympathy during the necessarily long period before the *bouleversement*. Fairy tale and pantomime can resort to caricaturing the heroine's oppressors. The serious novelist whose heroine must be unappreciated and neglected by a credible social world faces a harder problem.

It is solved in *Persuasion* partly by the dexterity of a practised writer, and partly through more mature understanding of the basic situation and the forms it may take. The vanity and shallow self-importance of Sir Walter Elliot and his eldest daughter, their heartless worldliness, accompanied by ill-judgment even in worldly things, are handled scathingly but with only a little caricature. The situation used to exemplify the clash between their values and Anne's – the problem of extravagance, debt and retrenchment – is more convincing to modern minds than the episode of the private theatricals in *Mansfield Park*. And the scales that were weighted too heavily against Fanny are being kept nearer level by the presence of Lady Russell, the influential friend, who not only sees Anne's worth (as Edmund did Fanny's) but is in many ways allied with her against the family and serves by her comments to indicate that people of good sense think as Anne does. Ill-health too is dealt with differently. Fanny's debility was presented almost as morally superior to the rude health of her companions. In *Persuasion*, which Jane Austen wrote when she was dying of a malady that gradually sapped her strength (resting on an arrangement of three chairs while her mother monopolized the sofa in the living room), it is the heroine's patience that has to be mustered to cope with the complaining hypochondria of her younger sister. Poor health is now as little a recommendation as it was in Miss De Bourgh in *Pride and Prejudice*. ('She looks sickly and cross – Yes, she will do for him very well.')

Of even greater importance than these changes of treatment is a more mature interpretation of the theme, one no longer presenting the heroine as a passive sufferer of entirely unmerited wrongs. Anne has brought her chief misfortune on herself through a mistaken decision – to break her engagement with Wentworth – to which she was persuaded by Lady Russell. Her lapse from her own standard, in letting worldly prudence outweigh love and true esteem for personal qualities, is the error which has also to be excused in her mother, who in marrying Sir

Walter was too much influenced by 'his good looks and his rank'. We start then with a much more mature Cinderella, more seriously tragic herself in having thrown away her own happiness, more complex in her relation to the loved mother, who not only made the same sort of mistake herself but now, brought back to life in Lady Russell, shares the heroine's responsibility for her disaster. Lady Russell is explicitly presented as the equivalent of a greatly loved mother, more nearly ideal than any other living mother that Jane Austen gives a heroine. In fairy tales the baffling intermingling of the hateful and loveable attributes of all mothers is simplified into a dichotomy between the ideal mother – entirely loveable, dead and beyond the test of mature observation – and the step-mother, living, entirely detestable and doing her worst for the child. In the maturity of *Persuasion* Jane Austen puts her heroine into relation with a lovable but not perfect mother who, in doing her mistaken best for the girl, has caused what seems an irremediable misfortune.

It is Wentworth's hurt feelings and his belief that Anne was over-yielding in giving him up that create the barrier between them when he comes back prosperous, seeking a wife and attracted by the amiable, commonplace Mus-grove girls. It is again Lady Russell, perceptive of Anne's worth though not of his, who provides a choric comment establishing the values. When Anne tells her about the apparent attachment between him and Louisa, 'Lady Russell had only to listen composedly, and wish them happy; but internally her heart revelled in angry pleasure, in pleased contempt, that the man who at twenty-three had seemed to understand somewhat of the value of an Anne Elliot, should, eight years afterwards, be charmed by a Louisa Musgrove.'

In fact, by the time this comment is made, the emotional barriers Wentworth had erected against Anne have been broken down in a graded sequence of incidents,

mingling observation and action on his part, which Jane
Austen manages with supremely delicate skill: at first, his
comment on Anne's altered looks, 'his cold politeness, his
ceremonious grace; then his inquiry of the others whether
she never danced (while she is playing for them to dance);
later, his quite unceremoniously kind and understanding
act in relieving her of the troublesome child, 'his degree
of feeling and curiosity about her' when he is told of her
having refused a more recent proposal of marriage, his
realizing her tiredness and insisting on her going home in
Admiral Croft's chaise ('a remainder of former sentiment,'
Anne thinks, 'an impulse of pure, though unacknowledged
friendship'); finally, his noticing the glance of admiration
she receives from Mr Walter Elliot at Lyme, followed
quickly by the climax of the accident on the Cobb and
the instant partnership between him and Anne as the
competent and responsible people keeping their heads in
a horrifying situation. From this point onward the tables
are turned; Captain Wentworth, in the full return of his
early love, has to face the anxieties of his apparent
commitment to Louisa and his jealousy at Mr Walter
Elliot's wooing of Anne. Although suspense and strong
emotion are maintained to the last pages, the visit to Lyme
is the turning point at which the earlier sadness – wasted
opportunity, regret, misunderstanding – has finally been
modulated with infinite skill into comedy.

It remains serious comedy. Captain Wentworth's release
from Louisa, it is true, has the arbitrariness of lighter
comedy; it recalls Edward Ferrar's release in *Sense and
Sensibility*. The serious problem lay in managing the
psychological terms on which the lovers came together
again. In the foreshortened ending of *Mansfield Park*,
Fanny waits passively for Edmund to recognize her full
value and transfer his wounded affections to her. Anne,
who actively caused the breach with Wentworth, must
take more than a passive part in its healing if she is to

remain consistently more responsible than the simpler Cinderella. It is in this light that the cancelled chapter must be seen. J.E. Austen-Leigh (*Memoir*, Chapter II) describes her dissatisfaction with it; she had come with failing strength to the end of the novel and had little resilience left for rewriting; yet she felt that the chapter in which she brought the lovers together was so unsatisfactory that the effort must be made. What was wrong with it?

It is in the style of lighter comedy. In a rather artificially contrived incident Admiral Croft compels Captain Wentworth to give Anne a message which assumes that she is to marry Mr Elliot. This obliges her to tell Wentworth that she is not intending to marry Mr Elliot, and Wentworth does the rest. Thus only an external event forces her to accept even the small part she does play in clearing up the misunderstanding. She is nearly as passive as Fanny. In the revised chapters (chapters 22 and 23) her role is much more active. The problem for Jane Austen was how to give her an active part in promoting the reconciliation without the impossible breach of decorum involved in telling him of her love, in effect proposing to him. The same problem had been met in *Pride and Prejudice* by Elizabeth's refusal to assure Lady Catherine that she would *not* refuse Mr Darcy. In the revised chapters of *Persuasion* the solution lies in Anne's making an almost public avowal, easily overheard in the crowded room, of her ideals of unchanging love and her belief that women have the unenviable privilege 'of loving longest, when existence or when hope is gone'. She could not have spoken like this if she had accepted Mr Elliot, and it tells Captain Wentworth enough. Like Elizabeth Bennet, she had not deliberately spoken to convey a message to him, but by standing up for her standards and openly avowing them she had played her active part in bringing her lover back again. The chapter goes on to emphasize still more the active responsibility she feels she must take; Wentworth having smuggled his ardent letter to her and gone, she has to make absolutely certain of giving him the word of encouragement he asks for. Her struggles to ensure this, in face of her friends' kind misunderstandings and ill-timed helpfulness, provide genial comedy, but none the less form part of the serious theme that distinguishes the revision from the cancelled chapter.

There is yet more of significance in the revision of the cancelled chapter, of significance for the central problem announced by the title of the novel – the rights and wrongs of Lady Russell's persuasion and of Anne's yielding. For all its general formulation the problem is embodied in the particular form created by the conflict between elderly prudence and the romantic love of two young people. The persuasion, or dissuasion, is exerted by an older person, disinterestedly concerned for the younger – but not in love; and the younger has to make up her mind. The novel was begun in 1815, and 150 years later the problem, in spite of an easier economic situation, is not unknown to girls of 19 and their mothers.

In Jane Austen's time and in her social class, the ideal of marriage for personal love rather than for an establishment or a family alliance was in a transitional stage. The theme occurs in several of her novels, most centrally perhaps in *Mansfield Park* and *Persuasion*, and her attitude is consistent: marriage without love is wrong. In 1802 she herself suffered great agitation through accepting a proposal of marriage from a well-to-do man and then the next day withdrawing her acceptance. In *Mansfield Park* she expressed herself ironically on out-and-out worldliness in Mary's description of the Frasers:

'I look upon the Frasers to be about as unhappy as most other married people. And yet it was a most desirable match for Janet at the time. We were all delighted.

She could not do otherwise than accept him, for he was rich, and she had nothing; but he turns out ill-tempered and *exigeant*; and wants a young woman, a beautiful young woman of five-and-twenty, to be as steady as himself . . . Poor Janet has been sadly taken in; and yet there was nothing improper on her side; she did not run into the match inconsiderately, there was no want of foresight. She took three days to consider of his proposals; and during those three days asked the advice of everybody connected with her, whose opinion was worth having; and especially applied to my late dear aunt, whose knowledge of the world made her judgment very generally and deservedly looked up to by all the younger people of her acquaintance; and she was decidedly in favour of Mr Fraser. This seems as if nothing were a security for matrimonial comfort!'

But at the other extreme what of an engagement where there is love but poverty? She is no less clearsighted: 'Wait for his having a living!' exclaims Mrs Jennings in *Sense and Sensibility*,

' – aye, we all know how that will end; – they will wait a twelve-month, and finding no good comes of it, will set down upon a curacy of fifty pounds a year, with the interest of his two thousand pounds, and what little matter Mr Steele and Mr Pratt can give her. – Then they will have a child every year! and Lord help 'em! how poor they will be! – I must see what I can give them towards furnishing their house.'

These are extremes. In *Persuasion*, on the other hand, the problem is posed without exaggeration or caricature and therefore in its most intractable form:

'Anne Elliot,' thinks Lady Russell, 'with all her claims of birth, beauty, and mind, to throw herself away at nineteen; involve herself at nineteen in an engagement with a young man, who had nothing but himself to recommend him, and no hopes of attaining affluence, but in the chances of a most uncertain profession, and no connexions to secure even his farther rise in that profession; would be, indeed, a throwing away, which she grieved to think of! Anne Elliot, so young; known to so few, to be snatched off by a stranger without alliance or fortune; or rather sunk by him into a state of most wearing, anxious, youth-killing dependance! It must not be, if by any fair interference of friendship, any representations from one who had almost a mother's love, and mother's right, it would be prevented.'

Some of the most interesting material in the revised chapters presents Jane Austen's attempt at an explicit answer to that problem, an enlargement and re-emphasis of what she had presented as Anne's opinion at the opening of the story. Here, however, in spite of some repetition (the extent of which she may possibly not have realized in this late revision), the answer is not without ambiguity. Once again, Anne is clear that she was right in yielding; it was a filial duty, and on that point there seems at first, as before, no question. Yet here she goes on immediately, in answer to Wentworth's question, to affirm that she would have renewed the engagement the following year if he had asked her when he returned to England 'with a few thousand pounds, and was posted into the Laconia'. His promotion to Captain, one profitable cruise in an old, worn-out sloop, and now a better posting, though it offered some promise would have been a weak answer to Lady Russell's full objections; and Jane Austen seems to imply that even a year's reflection and

regret would have lessened the filial submissiveness of a
girl like Anne. About Lady Russell's justification in the
advice she gave there is a more decisive answer than that
offered earlier. Then Anne did not blame her, though she
felt now that she would never have given such advice
herself. In the revised chapters the adverse judgment is
strengthened:

> 'I am not saying she did not err in her advice. It was,
> perhaps, one of those cases in which advice is good or
> bad only as the event decides; and for myself, I certainly
> never should, in any circumstance of tolerable similarity,
> give such advice.'

Such an explicit and extended recurrence to the theme
in her revised chapters brings out its importance to her
conception of the novel.

This is not a problem that stands isolated, either in
Persuasion or in her work as a whole; it is one outcome of
the intense, highly organized pressures of a close-knit
society. The functioning of individuals while they are
hemmed in by others, all mutually controlled by the
system of social forces, was one of her general preoccu-
pations. The small country neighbourhood, with little
travel, and no escape from the family by going to work in
a large organization, precluded the individual from having
the degree of anonymity we take for granted. He was, as
Henry Tilney remarks in *Northanger Abbey*, 'surrounded
by a neighbourhood of voluntary spies'. A characteristic
feature, of which Jane Austen makes very frequent use,
was the large party in the same drawing room, with the
possibility of private conversations in an undertone, sometimes overhead, sometimes concealed by the conversation
of others or the sound of the piano. Captain Wentworth
and Anne manage to have their discussion of their broken
engagement, and Lady Russell's part in it, during one of

their short contacts at an evening party, 'each apparently occupied in admiring a fine display of green-house plants'. And Captain Wentworth listens contemptuously to Mary's remarks after her snobbish sister has at last included him in her invitations:

> 'Only think of Elizabeth's including everybody!' whispered Mary very audibly. 'I do not wonder Captain Wentworth is delighted! You see he cannot put the card out of his hand.'

Whether too much semi-privacy and overhearing were really part of the drawing-room society of the period, they provide a constantly recurring device in Jane Austen's novels, almost as usual as the soliloquy on which the theatre of the period still relied. She was presumably exaggerating something that really went on. And her exploitation of it is not only a technical device for narrative and comment but a means of conveying her characteristic sense of the compressed social milieu, the criss-cross of unspoken awareness that marks a group of people in close contact and makes privacy, especially within the family, a precarious luxury.

Although these are the conditions of all that happens, Jane Austen's focus of interest is the survival and development of the private individual within them. The pressure of social contact may be escaped for brief intervals, as for instance when the heroine goes to her own room for 'reflection' – the half hour or so that allows her, after an agitating experience, to analyse her state of mind and bring order into her feelings before returning to the drawing room and playing her usual role. It is a way of life in which the more sensitive person can experience great isolation. Actual loneliness has its place in *Mansfield Park* and *Persuasion*, highlighted by the episode in each when, during the course of a walk, the heroine is left sitting alone while the others wander off. She remains involved with them (as spectator or overhearer) but left out of account by them, a figure of the Cinderella who turns novelist. Anne's detachment is presented again, within the framework of comedy, when she has to be confidante to both Mary and the Musgroves, sympathizing tactfully with the complaints of each about the others' household.

In such a society there are degrees of isolation. A high degree is created by the civil falsehood and polite evasion ('Emma denied none of it aloud and agreed to none of it in private') which break true social contact and leave the speaker in a position of tacit superiority but cut off from his hearers. So when Mary urges her sister to write home about the chance meeting with Mr Elliot, 'Anne avoided a direct reply, but it was just the circumstance which she considered as not merely unnecessary to be communicated, but as what ought to be suppressed.' And she deals similarly with the limitations of Admiral Croft, for whom she has real respect: 'Anne did not receive the perfect conviction which the Admiral meant to convey, but it would have been useless to press the enquiry farther. She therefore satisfied herself with commonplace remarks, or quiet attention, and the Admiral had it all his own way.'

A second degree of social detachment, less complete, occurs when the heroine recognizes an obligation to try to communicate but, met by stupidity or stubbornness, feels exempt from farther effort and lets things take their course, as Anne does when she has failed to open Elizabeth's eyes to Mrs Clay's design to marry their father. When every man is surrounded by a neighbourhood of voluntary spies what should be told and what suppressed becomes a matter for careful thought; a mistake in that calculation – about Wickham's character – is a pivotal point of *Pride and Prejudice*, and in *Persuasion* a similar problem about Mr Elliot confronts Mrs Smith.

A third form of insulation in this close-pressing society,

one implying less of superior detachment, is silently
accepted reticence between equals. It creates the tension
of confidence known to be withheld, but it remains social,
since neither person breaks off the relation by resorting to
deception or viewing the other clinically. In the much
earlier *Sense and Sensibility* the withheld confidence, the
'reserve', although respected, is a source of some distress
and mutual reproach for the sisters. In *Persuasion*, graver
and much less effusive, there has been complete silence
for several years between Anne and Lady Russell on the
subject of the broken engagement: 'They knew not each
other's opinion, either its constancy or its change, on the
one leading point of Anne's conduct, for the subject was
never alluded to.' The result is that Anne Elliot is
presented as self-contained, controlled and with hidden
power, in spite of her regrets and her real tenderness. She
has the quiet maturity of a sensitive individual who is loyal
to her own values without colliding needlessly and unprof-
itably with the social group she belongs to, or with people,
like Lady Russell, to whom, in spite of seeing their
limitations, she is deeply attached.

In so compact a civilized society, romantic love
between individuals who freely choose each other for
qualities not readily identified and categorized by those
around them is a disruption. It seems to offer escape from
that dependence on social support that discourages people
from resisting the expectations of their immediate group.
As Donne saw, the union of the two souls in love:

Defects of loneliness controules.

Lovers assuage their loneliness without paying the price of
full conformity. Whether the ideals of romantic love are
expressed in an attachment, like Anne's for Wentworth,
or in a refusal to marry for anything other than attachment,
like her resistance to the match with Mr Elliot, they

simultaneously express and support the individual's partial nonconformity, his selection from the values ruling around him. This aspect of romantic love relates it closely to Jane Austen's concern with the survival of the sensitive and penetrating individual in a society of conforming mediocrity.

Although the nucleus of the fable – Cinderella, the foundling princess – has its universal significance, there would be no novel unless it were embodied in a particular time and place, something realized more substantially than the sketchy never-never land of fairy tale and once-upon-a-time. In Jane Austen's society – as indeed in fairy tale – the girl who made an individual romantic choice might well have to defy the standards of class and social position. And in *Persuasion* the story is embedded in a study of snobbery, snobbery displayed amidst the sharply realized detail, social and physical, of life in country houses and Bath at the start of the Napoleonic wars. Jane Austen created the perfect starting point for her satire by giving Sir Walter Elliot a baronetcy, thus putting the family in a twilit region between the nobility and the gentry – still no more than gentry but distinguished among them by the hereditary title. His scorn for those beneath him and his anxious toadying to 'our cousins, the Dalrymples' who are of the nobility (Irish), provide a good deal of the astringent comedy of the book. By making him, moreover, financially embarrassed, she contrasts his pretensions, based on family and superficial elegance, with the solid security of the Musgroves, undistinguished landowners who look after their estates effectively, and of the families rising into social consequence on naval prize money. The querulous Mary, married into the Musgroves, carries on her struggle for precedence and proper attentions as a baronet's youngest daughter, and laments the impending disgrace of being connected, through her sister-in-law's marriage, with a family who actually farm. And Elizabeth, too, the eldest sister, has to come to terms with social dilution when she finally gives Captain Wentworth an invitation, realizing that in the conditions of Bath society a man of such distinguished bearing, whatever his forebears, will be an asset at her party. The standards that Anne has to resist are brought as close to her as possible by being shared in some degree even by Lady Russell, who 'had a value for rank and consequence, which blinded her a little to the faults of those who possessed them'.

Embodied and given life in the social realities of her own period, Jane Austen's satire still has currency in ours. The sense of the past which we need in reading it has two aspects, and the more familiar – the ability to enter into her social world and its outlook – counts for less than the other. The other is the ability to notice the people and the institutions of our own time on which her eye would have rested and her judgment been passed, and this means recognizing contemporary equivalents rather than seeking identities. We shall not look to Bath, then the last word in the contemporary, for parallels to Elizabeth Elliot's displaying, as part of her own distinction, the latest in domestic architecture and fashionable décor for giving parties. And if we look around us for Sir Walter Elliot, 'prepared', on his departure from Kellynch Hall, 'with condescending bows for all the afflicted tenantry and cottagers who might have had a hint to shew themselves', we may not find him now in many landed baronets. But we may be reminded of the story Lord Woolton tells of Mr Gordon Selfridge, whose room at the store was always filled with flowers on his birthday, contributed, as he said, by 'those dear little girls' – meaning the sales assistants and clerks: 'When, one day, I remarked on his good fortune, he asked whether my staff in Lewis's paid such testimony to me, and when I replied, "Never even a daisy", this naive character replied, "You ought to give them a hint."'
(Lord Woolton, *Memoirs*, London, 1959.)

At some points Sir Walter Elliot is touched with
caricature. His considered twofold objection to the navy,
for instance, as an occupation that may be 'the means of
bringing persons of obscure birth into undue distinction'
and one that also ruins the appearance has the exaggeration
that places him with such figures as Mr Collins and Lady
Catherine De Bourgh. But there is none of the mercy of
caricature in the measured severity of the final summing
up:

> Captain Wentworth, with five-and-twenty thousand
> pounds, and as high in his profession as merit and
> activity could place him, was no longer a nobody. He
> was now esteemed quite worthy to address the daughter
> of a foolish, spendthrift baronet, who had not had
> principle or sense enough to maintain himself in the
> situation in which Providence had placed him.

And there is more than caricature in Elizabeth who 'felt
her approach to the years of danger, and would have
rejoiced to be certain of being properly solicited by
baronet-blood within the next twelve-month or two'.
Then she would be able to take up her father's favourite
book, the Baronetage, 'with as much enjoyment as in her
early youth; but now she liked it not. Always to be
presented with the date of her own birth, and see no
marriage follow but that of a youngest sister, made the
book an evil; and more than once, when her father had
left it open on the table near her, had she closed it with
averted eyes, and pushed it away.' Although Elizabeth's
conceit makes her ridiculous, in her relations with Mr
Elliot and Mrs Clay for instance, she is no a figure of
simple comedy. She is presented seriously, as a disap-
pointed but cold-hearted and unlikeable young woman.
Like Sir Walter, she is handled by Jane Austen with
straightforward moral severity. When she faces the prob-

lem of entertaining the Musgroves on their unexpected visit to Bath:

> Elizabeth was, for a short time, suffering a good deal. She felt that Mrs Musgrove and all her party ought to be asked to dine with them, but she could not bear to have the difference of style, the reduction of servants, which a dinner must betray, witnessed by those who had been always so inferior to the Elliots of Kellynch. It was a struggle between propriety and vanity; but vanity got the better, and then Elizabeth was happy again.

But the explicit moral comment is rare. Mainly the appraisal is implicit in the detail of setting and event: Elizabeth, once mistress of Kellynch Hall, exulting in the two drawing-rooms in Camden Place; the anxious renewal of acquaintance with the Dalrymples after the lapse occasioned by the accidental omission of a letter of condolence; the bustle and talking in Molland's, 'which must make all the little crowd in the shop understand that Lady Dalrymple was calling to convey Miss Elliot'.

A fable of profound human significance, embodied in people, time, place, and social setting acutely observed, vividly conveyed, justly appraised – but still *Persuasion* would not be the novel it is without that management of tone which was an essential part of Jane Austen's superb equipment, an integral characteristic of her writing at its best. The triumph in *Persuasion* is the harmonizing of several attitudes, which could have been distinct and even discordant, into a complex whole. Foremost among them is Anne's grave tone of regret in her reconsideration of the problems of personal relation that centred around her yielding to Lady Russell; and later her gradual emergence from resignation to hope. With this goes the regretful clearsightedness with which she condemns the vanity of her family, an attitude consistent both with her filial objections and with the author's ruthless contempt for Sir Walter and his other children. Contempt is not an attitude Jane Austen shrank from; she gives it to Captain Wentworth, for instance, when he is the object of patronizing recognition by Anne's sisters. But in this novel it has to remain compatible with the good-humoured comedy found in the treatment of Admiral Croft, where genuine respect for his kindness and robust good sense is blended with amusement at his simplifications and lack of subtlety in matters of love and marriage. Recovering from his surprise at Captain Wentworth's not being to marry Louisa Musgrove, he laments that the Captain 'must begin all over again with somebody else. I think we must get him to Bath. . . . Here are pretty girls enough, I am sure. It would be of no use to go to Uppercross again, for that other Miss Musgrove, I find, is bespoke by her cousin, the young parson.' The tone is of good-humoured comedy. The robust simplifications are just exaggerated enough for every reader to be laughing a little at the Admiral, and yet there is an after-taste, for on reflection one notices that they exactly represent the level of personal and romantic discrimination that Jane Austen has shown to be characteristic of the Musgroves.

Appreciative as she is of their warmhearted family feeling, and sparing them the severity with which she treats the Elliots, she remains a detached observer of the limitations of such people as she represents in the Musgroves. One outcome of her detachment is the astringent handling of Mrs Musgrove's tearful laments about her dead son, Richard, a passage that has been criticized by people for whom Jane Austen's tough rationality in face of commonplace sentimentalism has been too much. Yet this passage is one of fine discrimination as well as toughness. The 'large fat sighings' of Mrs Musgrove are presented as ridiculous because her upsurge of lamentation

is for 'a thick-headed, unfeeling, unprofitable Dick Musgrove' who 'had been very little cared for at any time by
his family, though quite as much as he deserved; seldom
heard of, and scarcely at all regretted, when the intelligence of his death abroad had worked its way to Uppercross, two years before'. The mother's lamentation now is
sentimentalism. Even so, Captain Wentworth, who had
once had the troublesome boy under his command,
quickly controlled his scorn and entered into conversation
with Mrs Musgrove 'in a low voice, about her son, doing
it with so much sympathy and natural grace, as shewed
the kindest consideration for all that was real and unabsurd
in the parent's feelings'. The recognition that Captain
Wentworth, more intelligent, more sensitive, and more
mature than Mrs Musgrove, has the obligation of meeting
her on whatever ground they genuinely share is balanced
by the equally clear recognition that her emotion, though
sincere, is based on delusions she has elaborated in a couple
of days for the sake of having the emotion. The discriminations Jane Austen invites us to make allow her to claim
our appreciation of the Musgroves' warm friendliness and
delighted responsiveness to Captain Wentworth and at the
same time to insist on our recognizing how commonplace
and limited they are.

The mingling of tones is seen at its boldest in the
climax, the accident on the Cobb, where elements of
comedy are deliberately introduced into what is primarily
a scene of shock and anxiety and family disaster. Some
mis-readers have managed to ridicule the idea that a young
woman could be seriously injured by slipping off a few
steps, but in fact by impulsively jumping half a second
before the reluctant Wentworth is ready to catch her
Louisa launches herself on to her head on the stone quay
and receives a severe concussion. There is nothing
improbable about the seriousness of the accident or the
consternation and terror of her friends. But although this

gives the main note of the scene, the established character of her companions is used to bring in the overtones of comedy: Mary of course is hysterical and immobilizes her unfortunate husband, Henrietta faints and has to be supported by Anne and Captain Benwick, and Wentworth, desperate, is left with the real victim in his arms:

> 'Is there no one to help me?' were the first words which burst from Captain Wentworth, in a tone of despair, and as if all his own strength were gone.

The words are tragic but the tableau is comic, and after serious action has been taken and Benwick gone for a surgeon, the collapse of Mary and Henrietta is again used as a comic off-set to the real disaster:

> As to the wretched party left behind, it could scarcely be said which of the three, who were completely rational, was suffering most, Captain Wentworth, Anne, or Charles, who, really a very affectionate brother, hung over Louisa with sobs of grief, and could only turn his eyes from one sister, to see the other in a state as insensible, or to witness the hysterical agitations of his wife, calling on him for help which he could not give.

And then, when the isolated group of friends has to be brought back into contact with the wider world, Jane Austen allows herself for a moment her characteristic note of banter:

> By this time the report of the accident had spread among the workmen and boatmen about the Cobb, and many were collected near them, to be useful if wanted, at any rate, to enjoy the sight of a dead young lady, nay, two dead young ladies, for it proved twice as fine as the first report.

After this the high stress of the accident is eased off into the warmhearted care and generosity of the Harvilles, with the note of comedy sounding easily in their eager plans for somehow or other accommodating two or three more of the party in their tiny house.

For all its gravity and tenderness, *Persuasion* works within the convention of high comedy, like *Emma* and *Pride and Prejudice*. The inter-penetration of the various tones – severe satire, good-humoured comedy, appreciation of domestic affection, moral seriousness about personal relations and especially about love – is not merely a high development of skill in writing but reflects unity of conception and coherence of underlying values.

How far and in what ways *Persuasion* falls short of the novel Jane Austen would have written if she had been in full health can only be guessed at. It is not an unfinished novel, but by her standards it is short and there are hints towards the end of possible elaborations that were never carried out. It is about as long as the early *Northanger Abbey*, only about two thirds the length of *Sense and Sensibility* or *Pride and Prejudice*, and little more than half as long as *Mansfield Park* or *Emma*, the two novels which immediately preceded it.

The cancelled chapter indicates one way in which there might have been extensions. Had it stood, the novel would still have been complete, the outline unbroken, the story told, the characters and their pattern of interaction established. The revision brought not only the improvements that have already been discussed but substantial enlargement too, by the additional episode of the Musgroves' visit to Bath and the patterns of personal inter change which that allowed her to create. The Elliot snobbery, with Elizabeth's modified attitude to Captain Wentworth, is more fully exhibited, the good-natured confusion of a Musgrove gathering exemplified again, and Charles Musgrove's relations with his Elliot wife further illustrated. These enlargements repair no omission and correct no error of balance but, besides being entertaining in themselves, they enrich and strengthen the structure which has in essentials already been built. The same vitality and inventiveness, controlled within the main pattern, might presumably have amplified much of the latter part of the novel.

Possibly the revelation of Mr Elliot's character and past history is a problem that Jane Austen, given her earlier resources of physical energy, might have handled more enterprisingly (though Shakespeare found no better solution in *The Tempest*). But this is only one way in which the parts of the novel centring on Mr Elliot give an impression of something contemplated but not fully worked out. Though he is more villainous (a blacker villain than any other of Jane Austen's), his role is similar to Henry Crawford's in *Mansfield Park*; his charm is resisted by the morally perceptive Cinderella in spite of the attempted persuasion of her guardian figure, and the vanity of one of the Ugly Sisters allows him to lead her up the garden path. The two themes are given a much smaller part in this novel than in the earlier, and in particular Anne is not exposed to any persistent effort of persuasion from Lady Russell, who bides her time partly from caution and partly because Mr Elliot is still in mourning for his first wife. It may be that no more serious attempt at persuasion and no call for farther resistance by Anne would have formed part of a longer version, though it might well have done. What is much clearer, however, is that the tale of Mr Elliot's machinations is handled very cursorily and was never worked out in detail.

His main object was to prevent Sir Walter's remarriage and obviate the consequent threat to his own succession to the title. At the same time his attraction to Anne is shown as genuine, something quite other than the pretence with which he pays his attentions to her elder sister

in order to gain admission to the household and keep an
eye on the designing Mrs Clay. There are elements of
conflict here. For although in her winding up of the loose
threads Jane Austen suggest that as a son-in-law he would
have had his best chance of keeping Sir Walter single, his
marrying Anne would have so angered the deceived
Elizabeth who controlled the household that his admission
would have been on sufferance and his antagonism to Mrs
Clay would have confirmed Elizabeth in keeping her
there. In any case it is never clear what he could do to
prevent Sir Walter's marrying her, beyond encouraging
the snobbery that might oppose a 'degrading' connexion.
Her chances are as prosperous as ever up to the last, and
her throwing them up in order to become Mr Elliot's
mistress (with the very slender chance of eventual marriage) is left exceedingly improbable.

   That Jane Austen realized how poorly she had prepared
for this last disentanglement is evident from two features
of her revision of the cancelled chapter. One is the
overseen meeting of Mrs Clay and Mr Elliot when he is
supposed to be away from Bath, the first clear indication
of anything between them (though a very subtle hint has
been dropped earlier when Lady Dalrymple takes Miss
Elliot home from the shop in Milsom-street). The second
relevant feature of the revision is a little more puzzling –
the repeated and carefully emphasized postponements of
Anne's revelation to Lady Russell of Mr Elliot's deplorable
character. She meant to tell her at once – and had she in
fact done so it would have made no difference at all to the
novel as it now stands. And yet the importance of the
disclosure is stressed, and so is the fact of its being twice
delayed, first by the Musgroves' arrival ('but Anne convinced herself that a day's delay of the intended communication could be of no consequence'), and then by
her preoccupation with Captain Wentworth ('it became a
matter of course the next morning, still to defer her

explanatory visit . . . and Mr Elliot's character, like the Sultaness Scheherazade's head, must live another day'). This has all the air of preparing us for some development in the story of Mr Elliot's scheming for which the continued ignorance of Lady Russell as well as of Sir Walter and Elizabeth was essential. Possibly she was feeling her way towards the sort of sub-plot she had used in *Emma*, the immediately preceding novel, where she had presented full-blown the modern detective story technique of giving the reader all the clues and still misleading him. Whatever she had in mind would have meant elaborating much more carefully Mr Elliot's part in the plot, and that evidently involved a greater enlargement or revision of the novel than she could feel was worth undertaking, especially as earlier chapters would also need revision if the extended sub-plot were to be fully integrated with the main theme.

We are left with a slight puzzle, of the fascinating kind that creative work not quite completed will always offer. Not that *Persuasion* is an unfinished novel, as Henry James's *The Sense of the Past* is, for instance, or *The Last Tycoon* of Scott Fitzgerald. After all, she had told the story that essentially interested her and told it with all the richness of social setting and personal relation that make it a self-sustaining complex structure. She rightly judged that in *Persuasion* she had, as she wrote to her favourite niece four months before she died, 'a something ready for Publication'.

CHAPTER 9

Civil Falsehood in Emma

Without getting embroiled in difficulties about an author's intentions we can say that he must have some minimal expectations of what the reader will find in the work. Jane Austen must have expected any reader she was interested in to notice that *Emma* deals with a privileged and self-confident girl who has to learn from experience that she can make embarrassing and painful errors at points where she feels perfectly sure of herself and convinced of her good judgment. And a reader whom the author would appreciate further would notice that parts of the story concealed at a first reading – notably the secret engagement – are always hinted at by small clues, and that if he lets himself be deceived as Emma herself was his mistake arises from the way he interprets observable facts of the situation accurately reported, without any misstatements by the author; this technique (later familiar in the 'classical' detective story) is followed with such scrupulous discipline that it must have been a matter of forethought and deliberate care in the detail of the writing. But another concern that runs through the whole book can be more easily overlooked and may not have been fully thought out by Jane Austen although it is certainly a topic that preoccupies her as the novel develops. One aspect of it comes to the surface once or twice in explicit statement. The first occasion is lighthearted (though with strong irony at a second reading of the novel): Emma urges Frank Churchill, against his stimulated reluctance, to go with Mrs Weston and hear Jane Fairfax's new piano, but he demurs, saying that if it should turn out to have an indifferent tone he would be no support to Mrs Weston in making the best of it − 'I am the wretchedest being in the world at a civil falsehood'. 'I do not believe any such thing,' replied Emma, − 'I am persuaded that you can be as insincere as your neighbours, when it is necessary'. (It is of course a point at which Frank Churchill is being completely insincere to Emma.)

The second occasion of an explicit reference to the problem shows Emma explaining to herself the proviso 'when it is necessary' which justifies an insincerity of her own. Mr Weston has spoilt her plan for Box Hill by inviting Mrs Elton to join the party:

> Now, as her objection was nothing but her very great dislike of Mrs Elton, of which Mr Weston must already be perfectly aware, it was not worth bringing forward again; − it could not be done without a reproof to him, which would be giving pain to his wife; and she found herself therefore obliged to consent to an arrangement which she would have done a great deal to avoid; an arrangement which would probably expose her even to the degradation of being said to be of Mrs Elton's party! Every feeling was offended; and the forbearance of her outward submission left a heavy arrear due of secret severity in her reflections on the unmanageable goodwill of Mr Weston's temper.
>
> 'I am glad you approve of what I have done,' said he very comfortably. 'But I thought you would. Such schemes as these are nothing without numbers. One cannot have too large a party. A large party secures its own amusement. And she is a good-natured woman after all. One could not leave her out.'
>
> Emma denied none of it aloud, and agreed to none of it in private.

Self-restraint and polite concealment of this kind, however justifiable in some circumstances, inevitably involves treating the other person as inferior, someone for whom allowances have to be made, as for instance old people are listened to with simulated interest while they repeat oft-told stories. It is the most usual form of civil falsehood, one that Emma is shown as adopting in her dealings with the worthy bores of the place such as Miss Bates and even, with cautious distance, with the presumptuous vulgarity of Mrs Elton.

The discipline of withholding criticism, making allowances for dullness or weakness or oddity in friends is carried much further in the consideration given to the beloved father; the forbearance Emma gives Miss Bates as a rather tedious duty of civility she extends even further to Mr Woodhouse out of devotion and piety. However willingly she gives it, her indulgence of his whims and silliness is, like all such tactics, a derogation from his adult social significance. He has to be 'managed', not only by Emma but by all his friends. Mr Knightley, calling on business with Mr Woodhouse, turns to Emma 'as soon as Mr Woodhouse has been talked into what was necessary, told that he understood, and the papers swept away'. When the Coles' dinner invitation is being considered and Mrs Goddard is suggested as company for Mr Woodhouse that evening Mr Weston offers to 'step to Mrs Goddard in a moment, if you wish it':

> But the idea of anything to be done in a *moment*, was increasing, not lessening Mr Woodhouse's agitation. The ladies knew better how to allay it. Mr Weston must be quiet, and everything deliberately arranged.
>
> With this treatment Mr Woodhouse was soon composed enough for talking as usual.

'Treatment' is the apt word for a relation that has so much of the clinical in it. Without this forbearance the comfortable harmony of social intercourse is jangled. John Knightley is irritated into a sharp rejoinder to Mr Woodhouse's lamentations that he took his family to South End – his brother has to step in instantly to change the subject:

> 'Mr Woodhouse was rather agitated . . . but the soothing attentions of his daughters gradually removed the present evil, and the immediate alertness of one brother, and better recollections of the other, prevented any renewal of it.'

To John Knightley the troublesome rituals of sociability are irrational and exasperating:

> 'here are we setting forward to spend five dull hours in another man's house, with nothing to say or to hear that was not said and heard yesterday, and may not be said and heard again tomorrow. Going in dismal weather, to return probably in worse.'

But after their return through the snow he had recovered enough to join in the forms of civil falsehood that preserve companionable harmony: 'Mr John Knightley, ashamed of his ill humour, was now all kindness and attention; and so particularly solicitous for the comfort of her father, as to seem – if not quite ready to join him in a basin of gruel – perfectly sensible of its being exceedingly wholesome; and the day was concluding in peace and comfort to all their little party'.

When social peace and comfort are maintained through one person's making allowances and being forbearing the cost is the sacrifice of full personal equality. The active partner becomes like a mother with an overtired child, a nurse with a tetchy patient, a salesman, a diplomat at a reception. In fact this is Mr Knightley's objection when Emma imagines the yet unseen Frank Churchill as adapting his conversation easily to each acquaintance, talking to Mr Knightley of farming, to Emma herself of drawing or music – 'What! at three-and-twenty to be the king of his company – the great man – the practised politician, who is to read everybody's character, and make everybody's talents conduce to the display of his own superiority. . . . My dear Emma, your own good sense could not endure such a puppy when it came to that point'. Yet what is the alternative to some degree of polite insincerity and forbearance, making allowances, concealing boredom and irritation, in a small community where people have to go on meeting each other and minimizing the awkwardnesses created by differences in social standing and wealth, in intelligence, in education and cultural interests, in knowledge of the world; and sometimes in spite of serious quarrels? After the culmination of Emma's disastrous misunderstanding with Mr Elton about Harriet and herself she reflects:

> Their being so fixed, so absolutely fixed, in the same place, was bad for each, for all three. Not one of them had the power of removal, or of effecting any material change of society. They must encounter each other, and make the best of it.

Her one consolation is that none of them will speak about it and above all that her father need not know and be upset. She even has to admire the good sense that Mr Elton shows in contriving to go away for a few weeks; she has in fact had to enter into a reluctant and tacit alliance with Mr Elton to keep the secret. She pays the obligatory wedding visit, with Harriet, to the Eltons; she gives a dinner for them at Hartfield to preserve public appearances. And although her failure to respond to Mrs Elton's

over-familiar advances soon puts a distance between them
it remains a civil distance and they can always meet, as
she has foreseen that she and Harriet and Mr Elton
would have to meet 'in the common routine of acquaintance'.

Theirs is the kind of civil falsehood that in public
requires only mutual concealment of mutual dislike. Miss
Bates presents Emma with a much more complex problem
in social living. A 'great talker upon little matters . . . full
of trivial communication and harmless gossip', she 'exactly
suited Mr Woodhouse', and his problem was only how to
relieve her penury without seeming to offer charity and
threaten her status as a gentlewomen: 'It is a great pity that
their circumstances should be so confined! a great pity
indeed! and I have often wished – but it is so little that
one can venture to do – small, trifling presents, of anything
uncommon'. But to Emma, of higher intelligence, she
was hardly tolerable, 'so silly – so satisfied – so smiling –
so prosing – so undistinguishing and unfastidious – ', and
paying the occasional visit was a tedious duty. Mr Knightley, no less aware of her limitations, treats her kindly but
firmly, his conversation at the open window showing him
'most resolutely and commandingly' interrupting her flow
of chatter to ask his question, and keeping her to the
point about anything he could do for *her*, not Mrs Cole,
in Kingston. Emma is obliged to resort to more positive
civil falsehood all through the call during which Miss
Bates summarizes the letter announcing Jane Fairfax's visit.
Her compliments and simulated interest conceal the feelings that surface when she mimics Miss Bates in reply to
Mrs Weston's surmise that Mr Knightley might marry
Jane:

> 'How would he bear to have Miss Bates belonging to
> him? – To have her haunting the Abbey, and thanking
> him all day long for his great kindness in marrying Jane?

– "So very kind and obliging! – But he always had been such a very kind neighbour!" And then fly off, through half a sentence, to her mother's old petticoat. "Not that it was such a very old petticoat either – for still it would last a great while – and, indeed, she must thankfully say that their petticoats were all very strong."'

Not to conceal such feelings, to abandon civil falsehood, may do painful and unjustifiable damage to a social relation. Emma's efforts, so long sustained, to humour someone who was her inferior not only in material good fortune but in intellectual equipment and range of interest, finally breaks down into the frank and hurtful gibe on Box Hill, something for which she comes to feel much sharper remorse than any civil falsehoods and insincerities could have caused. Miss Bates is given a wounding glimpse of what has lain behind the sustained civilities of the past:

'Ah! – well – to be sure. Yes, I see what she means, (turning to Mr Knightley,) and I will try to hold my tongue. I must make myself very disagreeable, or she would not have said such a thing to an old friend.'

Miserable and contrite after Mr Knightley's severe rebuke, Emma makes a prompt call on Miss Bates as an implicit gesture of amends, and after an initial hesitation it is the decency and generous humility of Miss Bates ('she is only too good natured and too silly to suit me', as Emma has said in a more buoyant mood that allows her to accept Emma's renewed friendliness of approach and to return to the old relation, agreeing to trade again in the counterfeit coinage that makes for harmonious exchanges among members of the village community. And although Emma's civilities will always be less than spontaneous they are not altogether insincere, because beneath them is a genuine

respect for Miss Bates's good qualities; the relation is one
they both want to keep in spite of the difficulties it
presents in everyday intercourse. The extent to which
criticism and the frank expression of impatience should be
muted among acquaintances is a problem surviving beyond
the early nineteenth century.

Apart altogether from his sense of the special consideration due to Miss Bates on account of her vulner-
ability, Mr Knightley, whose integrity is one of the
touchstones of the novel, is always willing to practise the
degree of civil falsehood that consists in withholding
criticism that is not absolutely necessary. Trying to explain
Jane Fairfax's toleration of Mrs Elton's insolent familiarities
he says:

> 'Another thing must be taken into consideration too
> – Mrs Elton does not talk *to* Miss Fairfax as she speaks
> *of* her. We all know the difference between the pron-
> ouns he or she and thou, the plainest-spoken amongst
> us; we all feel the influence of a something beyond
> common civility in our personal intercourse with each
> other – a something more early implanted. We cannot
> give anybody the disagreeable hints that we may have
> been very full of the hour before.'

And he indicates his cool acceptance of the minor social
lubricants when, on setting off to see John and Isabella, he
asks Emma 'Have you anything to send or say, besides the
"love" which nobody carries?' His rebuke to the Eltons
by dancing with Harriet Smith at the ball is tacit. He is
firmness itself in checking Mrs Elton's presumptuous over-
familiarity when she wants to deliver his invitations to the
strawberry party at Donwell, but he does it with a half
joke that buffers the snub. And though to close friends –
Emma and Mrs Weston – he expresses his strong disapproval of her and says Harriet Smith would have been a

better wife for Elton, he has left her self-complacency so little disturbed that she can exclaim, on lamenting the news of his engagement:

> 'There would be an end of all pleasant intercourse with him. – How happy he had been to come and dine with them whenever they asked him! But that would be all over now. – Poor fellow! – No more exploring parties to Donwell made for *her*.'

It is the very fact that he has a low opinion of the Eltons that exempts him from the obligation of telling them so. With someone he fully values like Emma, someone who must accept her equality with him, without allowances being made, he pulls no punches. He is unsparing and offers no polite buffering, when he reproaches her on Box Hill. It is her lapse from one sort of civil falsehood, from the long sustained inhibition of impatient criticism, that he condemns.

The conflict between frankness and tact, between impulse utterance and considerate or prudent inhibition, was not to be solved by being non-committal, over-cautious in avoiding a false step, or excessively guarded in giving opinions; that policy led to the charge of being 'reserved', a term of more severe censure in Jane Austen's usage that it would be today, conveying something of our 'secretive'. In *Sense and Sensibility* Eleanor is startled and taken aback when Marianne throws back the reproach at her:

> 'Nay, Elinor, this reproach from *you* – you who have confidence in no one!'
>
> Elinor, distressed by this charge of reserve in herself, which she was not at liberty to do away, knew not how, under such circumstances, to press for greater openness in Marianne.

It is one of Emma's objections to Jane Fairfax that she is reserved, to which Mr Knightley replies:

> 'I always told you she was – a little; but you will soon overcome all that part of her reserve which ought to be overcome, all that has its foundation in diffidence. What arises from discretion must be honoured.'

Jane Fairfax's discretion turned of course to extreme wariness while her engagement was secret, with the result that Mr Knightley, talking with Emma and Mrs Weston, later mentions her increased reserve as a fault.

The opposed quality, the 'openness' that Elinor mentions in *Sense and Sensibility*, becomes a key concept in the later chapters of the novel while the dénouement proceeds. In these chapters the earlier preoccupation of the novel with Emma's self-education as she goes from one delusion and blunder to another is passed beyond. She has been painfully sobered. She gives only cautious sympathy on learning of Harriet's new infatuation (for Frank Churchill as she wrongly supposes); she makes genuinely contrite amends for the lapse on Box Hill; she accepts sadly but without resentment the rebuffs she meets with in trying to help Jane Fairfax; and she is quite clear about the limits of the interest she herself has ever felt in Frank Churchill. Her sober self-assessment is evident when she tells Mrs Weston she can hardly bear to be thanked by Jane Fairfax ' – for, oh! Mrs Weston, if there were an account drawn up on the evil and the good I have done Miss Fairfax – .' Her comment on John Knightley's letter of congratulation to his brother is as seriously humble as it is playful:

> 'He writes like a sensible man,' replied Emma, when she had read the letter. 'I honour his sincerity. It is very plain that he considers the good fortune of the engagement as all on my side, but that he is not without hope

of my growing, in time, as worthy of your affection, as you think me already. Had he said anything to bear a different construction, I should not have believed him.'

'My Emma, he means no such thing. He only means – '

'He and I should differ very little in our estimation of the two,' – interrupted she, with a sort of serious smile – 'much less, perhaps, than he is aware of, if we could enter without ceremony or reserve on the subject.'

In the same spirit, having told Frank Churchill there is a little likeness between them,

> 'If not in our dispositions,' she presently added, with a look of true sensibility, 'there is a likeness in our destiny; the destiny which bids fair to connect us with two characters so much superior to our own.'

And her sober self-assessment appears again when Mr Knightley has been praising Harriet's good qualities:

> 'Much of this, I have no doubt, she may thank you for.'
> 'Me!' cried Emma, shaking her head, – 'Ah! poor Harriet!'
> She checked herself, however, and submitted quietly to a little more praise than she deserved.

It had been as a more mature and chastened person that she had faced the knowledge that if Mr Knightley did marry Harriet Smith the disaster would be due to what she had done for the girl,

> and the only source whence anything like consolation or composure could be drawn, was in the resolution of

her own better conduct, and the hope that, however inferior in spirit and gaiety might be the following and every future winter of her life to the past, it would yet find her more rational, more acquainted with herself, and leave her less to regret when it were gone.

The last fifth of the novel deals with one surprise and disclosure after another: Jane Fairfax suddenly accepting the position with Mrs Smallridge, cancelled with the news of her engagement to Frank Churchill, Harriet not in love with Frank Churchill but with Mr Knightley, Emma's immediate realization that she herself was in love with Mr Knightley, Mr Knightley revealed as not in love with Harriet but with Emma, Harriet not desperately in love with Mr Knightley but going to marry Robert Martin after all – a clearing away of puzzles, secrets, misconceptions of character, mistakes, delusions about oneself and others. The idea of openness is first expressed by Mr Knightley in a conversation about Jane Fairfax with Emma and Mrs Weston, who have previously argued, Mrs Weston for, Emma against, the likelihood of his being in love with Jane. Saying nothing about their speculations they try indirectly to probe his feelings for her. When he praised her Emma ' felt that Mrs Weston was giving her a momentary glance; and she was herself struck by his warmth'. They get him to speak on, and Emma leads him to avow that he thinks very highly of her:

'And yet,' said Emma hastily, and with an arch look, but soon stopping – it was better, however, to know the worst at once – she hurried on – 'And yet, perhaps, you may hardly be aware yourself how highly it is. The extent of your admiration may take you by surprise some day or other.'
Mr Knightley was hard at work upon the lower buttons of his thick leather gaiters, and either the

exertion of getting them together, or some other cause, brought the colour into his face, and he answered,

'Oh! are you there! – but you are miserably behindhand. Mr Cole gave me a hint of it six weeks ago.'

He stopped. – Emma felt her foot pressed by Mrs Weston, and did not herself know what to think. In a moment he went on –

'That will never be, however, I can assure you. Miss Fairfax, I dare say, would not have me if I were to ask – and I am very sure I shall never ask her.'

Emma returned her friend's pressure with interest . . .

They encourage him to talk further of Jane and he criticizes her lack of openness,

Emma could not but rejoice to hear that she had a fault. 'Well,' said she, 'and you soon silenced Mr Cole, I suppose?'

'Yes, very soon. He gave me a quiet hint; I told him he was mistaken; he asked my pardon and said no more . . .'

Mr Cole may have been silenced but they are not and the surreptitious speculation goes on:

'Well, Mrs Weston,' said Emma triumphantly when he left them, 'what do you say now to Mr Knightley's marrying Jane Fairfax?'

'Why really, dear Emma, I say that he is so very much occupied by the idea of *not* being in love with her, that I should not wonder if it were to end in his being so at least. Do not beat me.'

The little scene juxtaposes Mr Knightley's expectation of openness with the covert communication of the two women through glances and foot pressures as they listen.

It is only as the dénouement proceeds that Emma is shown as the advocate of openness. In the first shock of hearing of the secret engagement, she exclaims in protest 'To come among us with professions of openness and simplicity; and such a league in secret to judge us all!' (Mrs Weston's report on first meeting Frank Churchill was carefully phrased: 'He appeared to have a very open temper – certainly a very cheerful and lively one'.) Later when Emma has finally established such good relations with Jane Fairfax as to be told in confidence of the plans she and Frank Churchill are making she expresses her appreciation with 'Oh! if you knew how much I love every thing that is decided and open!'

That heartfelt exclamation in favour of 'openness' might be taken as an irony or as a sign of her reformed outlook if at that point the reader remembered her past behaviour – her pretence of giving no advice while she ensured that Harriet would reject Mr Martin, her scheming about Harriet's portrait, her device for getting into the Vicarage and leaving Harriet and Mr Elton in the room alone, her secret speculations with Frank Churchill about Jane Fairfax and the Dixons. But the reader is not encouraged to remember this; Emma does not say, for instance, 'how much I have come to love'; she speaks rather as if it were an established part of her personality. And not long afterwards that impression is reinforced by her reflection that there will soon be no need to conceal anything from Mr Knightley and that she will be able to give him the full confidence 'which her disposition was most ready to welcome as a duty', a feature of her disposition not previously much in evidence. Rather than part of the self-correction that 'Emma' as an imagined person undergoes this love of openness looks more like a revision by Jane Austen of her conception of the persona, or if not a revision at least the development of an aspect of the persona that was only implicit in the earlier conception. It had to be developed if she were to marry Mr Knightly who had objected to Jane Fairfax as not having 'the open temper which a man would wish for in a wife'.

As these concluding chapters proceed, the possibility of openness, the alternative to civil falsehood which had remained in the background earlier, begins to command attention; and openness as an ideal is examined. To what extent can it be realized in civilized life and between what people? It is a more dominant interest here than in any other of Jane Austen's novels. Emma's private plans for Harriet Smith involved her almost from the beginning in secrecy and dissimulation, and she was not free from those trammels even in the first flush of joy at Mr Knightley's proposing. Like Mr Elton he too had been the object of Harriet's infatuation, and while Emma was feeling immense relief at knowing that he had felt nothing in return, 'there was time also to rejoice that Harriet's secret had not escaped her, and to resolve that it need not and should not'. The need to hold back the one secret leads to another; as she joyfully accepts Mr Knightley, Emma dare not confess that her earlier refusal to hear him sprang from the fear that he meant to speak of his wish to marry Harriet. That small blemish on the occasion leads to a general reflection from the author, a mature acceptance of a usual but not disastrous failure to achieve the ideal:

> Seldom, very seldom, does complete truth belong to any human disclosure; seldom can it happen that something is not a little disguised, or a little mistaken; but where, as in this case, though the conduct is mistaken, the feelings are not, it may not be very material.

It is only with the final comic miracle, when it has become clear that Harriet's labile sentiments are at last safely

anchored on Robert Martin, that Emma can look forward
to telling Mr Knightley the whole story:

> High in the rank of her most serious and heartfelt
> felicities, was the reflection that all necessity of conceal-
> ment from Mr Knightley would soon be over. The
> disguise, equivocation, mystery, so hateful to her to
> practise, might soon be over. She could now look
> forward to giving him that full and perfect confidence
> which her disposition was most ready to welcome as a
> duty.

Not only is the disposition that finds disguise and equivo-
cation so hateful greatly changed (partly by the character's
imagined reform, partly by the author's revision) from
what was displayed earlier, but the particular instance of
confidential disclosure is handled differently. Earlier in the
story Emma had observed the Eltons' unpleasant manners
towards Harriet and reflected that 'It was not to be
doubted that poor Harriet's attachment had been an
offering to conjugal unreserve.' The tone of distaste is
unmistakeable and we are not invited to criticize Emma
for it. But conjugal unreserve about Harriet's infatuation
with Mr Knightley is now seen as part of a welcome duty.
What matters, of course, is that Mrs and Mr Knightley
would respond very differently to the parallel disclosures;
openness as an ideal is less important than the quality of
the people sharing it.

An approach towards openness depends on shared
standards of civilized behaviour and is a sign of mutual
confidence that they are shared. Emma's relation with Jane
Fairfax is certainly not intimate, but in the final chapters
they are both made to feel that openness and mutual trust
are possible between them. Disclosing her plans Jane says
'And I will own to you, (I am sure it will be safe).' And
Emma has said she supposes Jane will be leaving the district

on her marriage ' – just as I begin to know you', cancelling their reluctant acquaintance since childhood. It is a scene of extraordinary foreshortening, in which a page and a half of text is enough for them to apologize to each other for their past behaviour and resolve on mutual forgiveness, for Emma to say she would have been tempted to speak about the engagement 'Had you not been surrounded by other friends' and for Jane to say how much she would have welcomed it, for Emma to ask after Frank Churchill and then to ask and be told about Jane's future plans. We can accept the suddenness and completeness of what is really a reconciliation in this very compressed scene. We accept it partly because we know that Emma has previously learnt to think much more highly of Jane Fairfax; 'She bitterly regretted not having sought a closer acquaintance with her, and blushed for the envious feelings which had certainly been, in some measure, 'the cause'. But more important, probably, is the immediately preceding scene in which they have been in tacit agreement in judging Mrs Elton's exhibition of ill-bred self-importance and jocular familiarity while she supposes that she is in the secret of the engagement and Emma is not:

> 'Not that I presume to insinuate, however, that *some* people may not think *you* perfection already. – But hush! – not a word, if you please.'
>
> It seemed an unnecessary caution; Jane was wanting to give her words, not to Mrs Elton, but to Miss Woodhouse, as the latter plainly saw. The wish of distinguishing her, as far as civility permitted, was very evident, though it could not often proceed beyond a look.

Emma and Jane Fairfax have in fact been in an unspoken partnership of civil falsehood, humouring Mrs Elton in her ridiculous display of social hamfistedness and self-satisfaction; Jane knows that Emma knows about the engagement and Emma knows that Jane knows she knows; they are allies in the civil falsehood that Mrs Elton's ill-bred sense of triumph forces on them. They slip away to a private exchange at their own level of civilized behaviour – which includes carefully avoiding any reference to what they feel for the people they have just escaped (Emma says she would have been tempted to refer to the engagement 'Had you not been surrounded by other friends'). The recognition that they are natural allies in an uncongenial social context had already been hinted at in the only other scene in which the novel brings them together privately – when at Donwell Abbey Jane Fairfax escapes from the strawberry gatherers and Mrs Elton's nagging insistence that she accept the delightful post of governess in Mrs Smallridge's family; she begs Emma to make her excuses when she is missed, refusing the offer of the carriage:

> 'I am fatigued; but it is not the sort of fatigue – quick walking will refresh me. – Miss Woodhouse, we all know at times what it is to be wearied in spirits. Mine, I confess, are exhausted. The greatest kindness you can show me, will be to let me have my own way, and only say that I am gone when it is necessary.'
> Emma had not another word to oppose. She saw it all; and entering into her feelings, promoted her quitting the house immediately, and watched her safely off with the zeal of a friend.

The effectiveness of the scene as Emma leaves the Bates's living room depends on our accepting a high degree of wordless communication between the two of them, an understanding based on the perception they both have that the other is a person of similar quality in understanding, education and interests, considerate behaviour, moral values, clear-sightedness about the need not to quarrel with people like Mrs Elton and (for different reasons) to make allowances for people like Miss Bates and Mr Woodhouse; though they both feel remorseful about their past behaviour they recognize tacitly, however intolerable it would be to say so, that they are of better civilized quality than most of the people around them. Between them there could be openness; between each of them and most of those they have to meet and live with there has to be some kind and some degree of civil falsehood. Emma is left with Mr Knightley as the one person with whom she can hope to be fully open, and Mrs Weston with whom she can share many confidences though silencing her criticism of Mr Weston; for the rest she and Mr Knightley have to follow the practice of making allowances, humouring, being civil, limiting equal personal contact to the areas in which they can genuinely respect the other person, whether Mr Woodhouse, the Coles, Miss Bates or Harriet, and even keeping on such terms with the Eltons that clashes are avoided and parish business conducted so smoothly that Mrs Elton can continue to proclaim that Mr Elton is Knightley's right hand.

CHAPTER 10

Fraternal and Conjugal Love
(Fanny Price and Edmund)

If we give too much attention to Jane Austen's remark to Anna Austen (in her letter of 9 September 1814) that in fiction '3 or 4 Families in a Country Village is the very thing to work on' we may not notice that a major achievement of *Mansfield Park* consists in bringing a wide range of diverse social milieux into effective relation with one another, not just recording them as social facts but illuminating their styles and standards by individual contacts that bring out their merits and decencies, their limitations of moral outlook, their possibilities for mutual liking, their clashes and incompatibilities: the Mansfield Park family together with their social equals the Rushworths; the lower order of gentlefolk represented by the Norrises and the Grants at the parsonage; the sophisticated Regency world of the Crawfords, with the Admiral and his mistress, the Stornaways and Frasers, and the dubious friends Tom Bertram has made; the almost submerged Mrs Price reduced to a squalid house, a coarse husband in the lower ranks of the navy, in which a promising but unprivileged son hopes to make his difficult way to a better position than his father's. These worlds are at times brought into direct contact with each other, but the essential link among them, and the percipient judge of them all, is Fanny Price. That vital role of hers adds to our uneasiness at not feeling the liking for her as a heroine which Jane Austen seems to invite. What liking or sympathy we feel is certainly not unalloyed. The position is quite different from that of *Emma* in which the reader can share the author's view of a faulty heroine who has to learn from her mistakes and reform; Fanny has no need to reform, only to wait until her fine qualities are perceived by the reformed judgment of those around her. She is not easy to take to.

It may seem that the difficulty lies in accepting without demur her almost impregnable rightness. Her moral rules are as firm as Sir Thomas's and firmer than Edmund's, her observations of other people more alert and sensitive than either of theirs (notably in what she sees of the relations among Maria, Julia, Mr Rushworth and Henry Crawford), and her social and moral judgments are sounder than theirs. She verges on the priggish. And yet in this moral firmness and impeccable judgment she is at least equalled by Elinor in *Sense and Sensibility*; every reader must wince when Elinor supervises her mother and Marianne in their penitent recognition of their ill-judged conduct towards Willoughby, each eager for the greater blame. Marianne concludes:

'I have nothing to regret – nothing but my own folly.'

'Rather say your mother's imprudence, my child,' said Mrs Dashwood; '*she* must be answerable.'

Marianne would not let her proceed; – and Elinor, satisfied that each felt their own error, wished to avoid any survey of the past that might weaken her sister's spirits.

and changes the subject. Yet in spite of this kind of thing Jane Austen can still win our sympathy for the character as a whole, especially in presenting Elinor's dignity and courage in coping with Lucy Steele while she comes to terms with the shattering news of Edward Ferrars' secret engagement. She and Fanny Price have in common the distress of seeing the man they love apparently committed to another woman and one unworthy of him (vastly superior though Mary Crawford is to Lucy Steele).

A further element making it hard to like Fanny is perhaps the over-emphasis on her poor physique and doubtful health; she is not strong, has weak nerves (compared with her sister Susan at 14), suffers from headaches, all borne with an uncomplaining patience that puts at a moral disadvantage the robust members of the household who use her as a drudge and take it for granted that she should not share their privileges. She is (to use a crude and not very accurate label) a Cinderella figure. But so is Anne Elliot in *Persuasion*, and there Jane Austen presents the same basic idea in a way that never risks forfeiting our respect. Anne too is disregarded, excluded from the annual visit to London, left to cope with all the troublesome chores that the letting of Kellynch Hall involves, claimed unceremoniously as a nurse-companion when her younger sister feels unwell; but she retains dignity (partly through Lady Russell's appreciation of her), and the effect of her broken engagement on her health is not overstated, though formidable in its significance – she has lost her youthful bloom and at her age has little prospect of a marriage that Lady Russell can view as worthy of her. She is a much more maturely imagined version of a heroine undervalued by her family. If Fanny Price had been the later creation she would surely have seemed a retrograde sentimentalizing of a Cinderella, her ill-health used to load the dice in her moral favour. Yet as a heroine she might well have survived this in view of the impression she is allowed to make of mature resilience after the shock of being plunged back into her Portsmouth family – she sees Susan's possibilities and sets about developing them, she subscribes to the circulating library, she keeps her head (with an intense effort) in introducing Crawford to the family who cause her so much shame, and though he sees that life in her family home has affected her looks, this only adds to his concern without diminishing her attractiveness. She is no longer the wilting person with a headache whom Mrs Norris scolds for lying unnoticed on the sofa.

Like her ill-health, Fanny's timidity and shrinking seem to call so confidently for sympathy that we may withhold it. She seems self-destined to be wronged by the selfish and self-confident. This is not the impression that the opening chapters give; nothing but the sort of sympathy invited by Jane Austen is to be felt in viewing the frightened 10-year-old coming as a socially inferior dependent to a great house, uncertain, submissive, looked down on; and then timidly but gladly accepting the practical help that Edmund, more sensitive than the rest of the family, discovers that she needs. In these first three chapters, almost a prologue to the real action, she is presented quite clearly as an involuntary sufferer. It is after Sir Thomas's departure for Antigua, when she is sixteen, that she seems with too much willingness to embrace the role of family nonentity. When Tom urges her to act Cottager's wife he tries to overcome the timidity that he assumes to be her only objection by telling her the part is very small 'and it will not much signify if nobody hears a word you say, so you may be as creepmouse as you like'. Although his remark opens the social bombardment that puts the reader firmly on Fanny's side, his phrase – as creepmouse 'as you like' – tempts us to sympathize with his robust irritation; and without being sure that Jane Austen means us to. Fanny comes too near relishing the role of being downtrodden.

Her readiness to suffer in silence while most of the family treat her inconsiderately gives all the greater relish to her enjoyment when Edmund comes to the rescue to save her from the worst impositions and bring help or at the very least feel anxious (and sometimes self-reproachful) concern about their effect on her health. With William's arrival for a visit 'Fanny had never known so much felicity in her life' – 'Excepting the moments of peculiar delight, which any marked or unlooked for instance of Edmund's consideration of her in the last few months had excited'. She is very firmly lodged in his conscience:

> Edmund said no more to either lady; but going quietly to another table, on which the supper tray yet remained, brought a glass of Madeira to Fanny, and obliged her to drink the greater part. She wished to be able to decline it; but the tears which a variety of feelings created, made it easier to swallow than to speak.
>
> Vexed as Edmund was with his mother and aunt, he was still more angry with himself. His own forgetfulness of her was worse than anything which they had done.
>
> Fanny went to bed with her heart as full as on the first evening of her arrival at the Park. The state of her spirits had probably had its share in her indisposition; for she had been feeling neglected, and been struggling against discontent and envy for some days past. As she leant on the sofa, to which she had retreated that she might not be seen, the pain of her mind had been much behind that in her head; and the sudden change which Edmund's kindness had then occasioned, made her hardly know how to support herself.

Her ailing condition brings its oblique satisfactions, all the more oblique in that the attention Edmund gives her in a brotherly spirit brings a secret gratification to her more than sisterly feelings for him.

Fanny's feelings have changed from those of the dependent cousin who has gradually come to be treated by Edmund (though not by the rest of the family) as if she were a young sister. Her gratitude for the protective affection of an older brother changes in time to the longing to possess this knight errant as a husband. But there are uncertainties and ambiguities in the way the change is indicated and the degree of her own commitment:

> It was her intention, as she felt it to be her duty, to try to overcome all that was excessive, all that bordered on selfishness in her affection for Edmund . . . To think of him as Miss Crawford might be justified in thinking, would in her be insanity . . . She would endeavour to be rational, and to deserve the right of judging Miss Crawford's character and the privilege of true solicitude for him by a sound intellect and an honest heart.
>
> She had all the heroism of principle, and was determined to do her duty; but having also many of the feelings of youth and nature, let her not be much wondered at if, after making all these good resolutions on the side of self-government, she seized the scrap of paper on which Edmund had begun writing to her, as a treasure beyond all her hopes, and reading with the tenderest emotion these words, 'My very dear Fanny, you must do me the favour to accept' – locked it up with the chain, as the dearest part of the gift. It was the only thing approaching to a letter which she had ever received from him: she might never receive another; it was impossible that she ever should receive another so perfectly gratifying in the occasion and the style.

– so far we are being invited, at least in the main, to sympathize with Fanny; but as the passage goes on Jane Austen uses a hint of mockery to establish a slight distance:

> Two lines more prized had never fallen from the pen of the most distinguished author – never more completely blessed the researches of the fondest biographer. The enthusiasm of a woman's love is even beyond the

biographer's. To her, the hand-writing itself, independent of any thing it may convey, is a blessedness. Never
were such characters cut by any other human being, as
Edmund's commonest hand-writing gave! This speci-
men, written in haste as it was, had not a fault; and
there was a felicity in the flow of the first four words,
in the arrangement of 'My very dear Fanny,' which she
could have looked at for ever.

In her next novel Jane Austen caricatured and frankly
ridiculed the same sort of behaviour in Harriet Smith's
hoarding of her 'Most precious treasures', the bit of
sticking plaster Mr Elton has fingered and the leadless stub
of pencil he threw away. Both girls are yearning towards
someone they hardly dare love. She is handling Fanny
Price much more gently of course, but the touch of
mockery signals her sense of the less than mature quality
of Fanny's love.

The difficulty of knowing quite what to feel about
Fanny's love is increased by the fact that much of her
distress, as the novel presents it, could be simply the
unhappiness of an unmarried sister at seeing a brother
infatuated with a girl she thinks unworthy of him and is
also jealous of in the way that such a sister easily may be.
Suggestions that Fanny's love for Edmund goes beyond
the sisterly are brought in gradually once Mary Crawford
has appeared, but they are sometimes slightly ambiguous
or indefinite, notably in the passage about William's visit
to Mansfield Park:

Excepting the moments of peculiar delight, which
any marked or unlooked-for instance of Edmund's
consideration of her in the last few months had excited,
Fanny had never known such felicity in her life, as in
this unchecked, equal, fearless intercourse with the
brother and friend, who was opening all his heart to her

... and with whom (perhaps the dearest indulgence of the whole) all the evil and good of their earliest years could be gone over again, and every former united pain and pleasure retraced with the fondest recollection. An advantage this, a strengthener of love, in which even the conjugal tie is beneath the fraternal. Children of the same family, the same blood, with the same first associations and habits, have some means of enjoyment in their power, which no subsequent connections can supply; and it must be by a long and unnatural estrangement, by a divorce which no subsequent connection can justify, if such precious remains of the earliest attachments are ever entirely outlived. Too often, alas! it is so. – Fraternal love, sometimes almost every thing, is at others worse than nothing. But with William and Fanny Price it was still a sentiment in all its prime and freshness, wounded by no opposition of interest, cooled by no separate attachment, and feeling the influence of time and absence only in its increase.

It is a curious passage, in which the author's general reflections (no doubt connected with her personal experience, though that is not relevant here) have added some confusion to what is in any case an uncertain account of Fanny's feelings: the opening sentence implies, in her superior delight in Edmund's kindness to her, at least the beginning of an attachment, while the last sentence denies there being any separate attachment to cool her sentiment for William. One could argue that 'attachment' means something stronger or more definite than what Fanny felt for Edmund, but that will hardly do, for later on, without any change in her feelings or her relation to Edmund, it is her secret love and commitment to him that create the most formidable obstacle to Henry Crawford's hopes – 'He knew not that he had a pre-engaged heart to attack. Of *that*, he had no suspicion'.

A more disengaged view of the relations between grown-up sisters occurs in the account of Mrs Price's perfunctory concern about Lady Bertram's troubles:

> So long divided, and so differently situated, the ties of blood were little more than nothing. An attachment, originally as tranquil as their tempers, was now become a mere name. Mrs Price did quite as much for Lady Bertram, as Lady Bertram would have done for Mrs Price. Three or four Prices might have been swept away, any or all, except Fanny and William, and Lady Bertram would have thought little about it.

It is the brother-sister attachment whose lastingness is asserted with such strong conviction. Although during the coach journey to Portsmouth Fanny and William are being playful in their fantasies about his rapid rise in the navy, it remains consistent with the sort of relation already suggested that his prize money 'was to be generously distributed at home, with only the reservation of enough to make the little cottage comfortable, in which he and Fanny were to pass all their middle and later life together.'

The brotherly feeling for a cousin brought up in the home, which Mrs Norris rightly predicted, has in Edmund remained what it was. And Jane Austen so effectively conveyed the sisterly feeling in Fanny for a kind and protective and adored older brother that its replacement by other feelings was inevitably difficult to handle; it had from early on held a quality not fully recognized and certainly not reciprocated by the brother, but still not unknown in sisters. As she watches Edmund growing absorbed in Mary Crawford, Fanny has the sense of loss and the unadmitted jealousy that commonly await an emotionally dependent sister when the brother attaches himself to another girl. Though she sees that as only too understandable she still longs for the earlier time and the old unrivalled possession of the affectionate brother – and we have the scene in which Fanny nearly inveigles Edmund back into the old pursuit of gazing at the stars and learning to identify them, only to see him at the last moment fascinated by Mary and moving to join the group with whom she has been singing. Here, and in her patient suffering as he deprives her of her ride in order to give longer to Mary's remarkable promise as a horsewoman, the picture could be of a sister's muted jealousy and resigned regret, sharpened by and sharpening her perception of Mary's faults. We are given no sign that she admits to herself at this time what her feeling are: even her jealous agitation at watching Edmund and Mary rehearsing for *Lovers' Vows* could still be compatible with the same sisterly distress; it is not until the episode of receiving Edmund's gift of a gold chain that she is shown explicitly as admitting to herself that she is tempted 'To think of him as Miss Crawford might be justified in thinking' and then she reprobates the thought as insanity and resolves not to give way to it (though treasuring the scrap of his unfinished letter). Nothing reported of her self-awareness corresponds to Anne Elliot's or Elinor Dashwood's clear recognition of their feelings as they face the loss of a lover.

This slightly uncertain quality of Fanny's love as it emerges from, or distinguishes itself as, brotherly affection have their effect on the climactic interview when Sir Thomas tries to probe her resistance to Henry Crawford's proposal and finally upbraids her mercilessly. Her emotional stress in concealing her love for Edmund is stated rather than presented. Sir Thomas's interrogation on this point, calculated and indirect with a subtlety we are not prepared for from him, presents some threat to her secret; but while he ponders his approach Fanny is 'trying to harden and prepare herself against farther questioning.

She would rather die than own the truth, and she hoped by a little reflection to fortify herself beyond betraying it.' And when Sir Thomas works round to his deliberated question – whether she agrees that Edmund would like to marry Mary Crawford – she replies:

> 'Yes, Sir.'
> It was gently, but it was calmly said, and Sir Thomas was easy on the score of the cousins.

The quietness, almost flatness of the interchange contrasts sharply with the scene in *Sense and Sensibility* in which Elinor has to shield her secret love for Edward from Lucy Steele's suspicious probings; there the writing leaves no doubt of the tension and of Elinor's struggle for control. The intense emotion of the scene with Sir Thomas is evoked only by his reproaches for her ingratitude. Again, Fanny looks forward with terror to the farewell interview with Mary Crawford, who is full of her brother's love for Fanny and of Edmund's for herself:

> As a sister, so partial and so angry, and so little scrupulous of what she said; and in another light, so triumphant and secure, she was in every way an object of painful alarm. Her displeasure, her penetration, and her happiness were all fearful to encounter.

At the end of their talk 'she had escaped without reproaches and without detection. Her secret was still her own; and while that was the case, she thought she could resign herself to almost everything.' But though her relief is in this way stated, she has not at any point in the discussion been made to feel in danger. Mary is entirely frank (though of course not explicit) in conveying what she felt about Edmund; unlike Lucy Steele she has no suspicion that she may be talking to a rival, and Fanny's secret is so safe that the scene lacks tension and tautness. Her role as a 'sister' has been too fully established for Mary, or Edmund himself, to see her in any other light, and Sir Thomas's incipient suspicion is easily allayed. Where the complication of the sisterlike role is absent Jane Austen is perfectly well able to convey her other heroines' sexual love, whether it shows itself in a sudden change, as it does with Elizabeth Bennet and still more overwhelmingly with Emma, or develops gradually and quietly as in Elinor, or remains as a grief like Anne Elliot's.

For Edmund the brother-sister relation remains unchallenged throughout the novel proper (excluding the last chapter, when loose ends are tied off). It is the brother-sister relation at its closest that unites him with her when he arrives in Portsmouth in the depths of the family's misery, with Tom very possibly dying, Maria hopelessly disgraced, and Julia, it seems, equally lost to them through her elopement with a discreditable young man. Fanny goes down to the parlour on his arrival:

> He was alone, and met her instantly; and she found herself pressed to his heart with only these words, just articulate, 'My Fanny – my only sister – my only comfort now.'

And it is still as if she were his sister, his only comfort, that he describes his last meeting with Mary Crawford and the finality of the breach between them.

In effect the novel ends at this point, its slowly mounting dramatic conflict decided. Edmund's rejection of Mary is the final collision between the two major social milieux that Jane Austen brings into contact. It might be tempting to call it a conflict between the sober respectability of Mansfield Park and the spontaneity and moral carelessness of the society identified with the Regent. But that would imply a very false idealization of Mansfield Park: the society there includes not only Edmund and Fanny with the principles that guide them, but Maria and Julia, Mrs Norris, Lady Bertram, Tom with his dubious friends before illness sobered him, and in spite of his respectability Sir Thomas's own failings as a father and his too easy acceptance of a convenient alliance with the stodgy and stupid Rushworths who are acceptable neighbours in the country society of which Mansfield Park forms part. Nothing in the novel leads us to reject the Crawfords' appraisal of the family: Henry has been revelling in what he will do for Fanny when she is freed 'from all the demands of her aunt's stupidity', and when, he hopes, Maria and Julia 'may be heartily ashamed of their own abominable neglect and unkindness'; he will give her:

> 'the consequences so justly her due, Now she is dependent, helpless, friendless, neglected, forgotten.'
> 'Nay, Henry, not by all, not forgotten by all, nor friendless or forgotten. Her cousin Edmund never forgets her.'
> 'Edmund – True, I believe he is (generally speaking) kind to her; and so is Sir Thomas in his way, but it is the way of a rich, superior, longworded, arbitrary uncle.'

Earlier it has been Mary who sees Mrs Norris's venomous comment on Fanny's refusal to act in the play as an outrage. The Crawfords' view of much in Mansfield Park is not one that we are asked to reject.

The central clash in the novel is not between the Crawfords and Mansfield Park but between their standards and those represented by Fanny's insight and firm disapproval – that of the established church given revived seriousness by the challenge of the 'evangelicals' of the period – which Edmund shares with her as long as he is not under Mary's spell, and which Sir Thomas has in the upshot to ally

himself with when the Crawfords' standards are unequivo-
cally displayed. When Mary Crawford, hoping to patch
together some shreds of respectability for Maria after the
elopement with Henry, is disconcerted and shocked by
Edmund's horror at realizing that she sees it as a social folly
rather than a 'dreadful crime', she turns her dismay and
anger into derision, pointing up and exaggerating the evangelical in him:

> 'A pretty good lecture upon my word. Was it part of
> your last sermon? At this rate, you will soon reform
> every body at Mansfield and Thornton Lacey; and when
> I hear of you next, it may be as a celebrated preacher in
> some great society of Methodists, or as a missionary into
> foreign parts.'

Jane Austen's letters show her effort to be fair to the
evangelicals and her effortless dislike of them. She teased
Cassandra by being prejudiced in advance against Hannah
More's *Coelebs*:

> My disinclination for it before was affected, but now it
> is real; I do not like the Evangelicals. – Of course I shall
> be delighted, when I read it, like other people, but till I
> do I dislike it. (*Letters*, 24 January 1809)

Later on, while skilfully avoiding (as always) any direct
advice to Fanny Knight on her current young man, she
refused to admit:

> any objection from his *Goodness*, from the danger of his
> becoming even Evangelical, I cannot admit *that*. I am by
> no means convinced that we ought not all to be Evan-
> gelicals, & am at least persuaded that they who are so
> from Reason and Feeling, must be happiest & safest.
> (*Letters*, 18 November 1814)

Seven years later, in contact with the work of her evangelical cousin Edward Cooper, her antipathy was clear:

> We do not much like Mr Cooper's new Sermons: –
> they are fuller of Regeneration & Conversion than ever
> – with the addition of his zeal in the cause of the Bible
> Society. (8 September 1816)

His was the socially intrusive kind of evangelicalism, creating embarrassment for people who had no wish either to reject his good principles or share in his fervour.

For the soberly pious Christian like Fanny Price a more acceptable expression of deep religious conviction, less disturbing to ordinary social intercourse, was offered in some of Cowper's poetry, especially in passages where intelligent wonder at the marvels of nature conveyed the awe inspired by their creator:

> What prodigies can power divine perform
> More grand than it produces year by year . . .
> All we behold is miracle, but seen
> So duly, all is miracle in vain.
> Where now the vital energy that moved,
> While summer was, the pure and subtle lympth
> Through the imperceptible meandering veins
> Of leaf and flower? It sleeps; and th'icy touch
> Of unprolific winter has impress'd
> A cold stagnation on the intestine tide.
> But let the months go round, a few short months,
> And all shall be restored. These naked shoots,
> Barren as lances, among which the wind
> Makes wintry music, sighing as it goes,
> Shall put their graceful foliage on again,
> And more aspiring, and with ampler spread,
> Shall boast new charms, and more than they have lost.
> (*The Task – The Winter Walk at Noon*)

It is this spirit of reverently intelligent wonder that Fanny emulates (though without the explicit religious reference) in her offerings to the conversation with Mary Crawford in the Grants' shrubbery. She has tried the miracle of memory without getting a response from Mary, so she turns to the subject of evergreens:

> The evergreen! How beautiful, how welcome, how wonderful the evergreen! When one thinks of it, how astonishing a variety of nature! − In some countries we know the tree that sheds its leaf is the variety, but that does not make it less amazing that the same soil and the same sun should nurture plants differing in the first rule and law of their existence. You will think me rhapsodizing; but when I am out of doors . . .

Mary replies with a light touch, confessing in confidence that previously she 'had not imagined that a country parson ever aspired to a shrubbery or anything of the kind', and that to her, like the Doge at the French court, the greatest wonder of the place was to find herself in it. It may be that Fanny's exploratory interest in psychology and botany promises more lasting enjoyment than Mary's lighthearted comment, but they come ominously close to the style Jane Austen had laughed at in Mary Bennet. And in the whole of the shrubbery conversation it is Mary Crawford, seemingly so sophisticated, who is really the much more naive, forthcoming and trustful in her confidences, without the least suspicion that Fanny sees her as a rival and deeply disapproves of her moral outlook. In reading the passage one must find it difficult to prefer Fanny's personal standards on the whole to Mary's, or to feel sure whether or not Jane Austen did.

In Jane Austen's period the Regency outlook and style of behaviour, though widely condemned for its sexual laxity, was still in the open and could be admired for its lightness of touch and range of interest; the final rejection of the Crawfords by Edmund and Fanny, with the relinquishment of their gaiety and alert hedonism, paralleled the process that would change Regency into mid-Victorian, also with losses; Fanny Knight, who had once delighted Jane Austen by trying to excite her doubtful feelings for one young man by a visit to his room, where she met with his dirty shaving rag, became the second Lady Knatchbull whose letter (quoted by Tucker, pp. 193–4) about Jane and Cassandra Austen's lack of refinement plumbs scarcely believable depths of contemptible snobbery; the disparagement of her aunts is not remarkable (there are signs of unpleasant traits in her character as a girl) but to suppose that what little they did know of good society and refinement depended on what they met through their brother Edward who had become a wealthy landed gentleman by adoption – this is a degree of complacent obtuseness worthy of Lady Bertram and Mrs Rushworth. It was the Rushworth standards that came out on top by the mid-century when the Regency style of sexual behaviour had been forced underground. The Crawfords are rejected not by 'Mansfield Park' but by Fanny's insight and judgment regretfully recognized in the end by Edmund and belatedly endorsed by Sir Thomas.

The climax created by Edmund's rejection of Mary Crawford is not at the same time the triumph of Fanny's love for him; it leaves her only with the satisfaction of a sister who sees a brother saved from an unworthy woman, the fraternal tie unthreatened by the conjugal. Edmund's conversation into a lover is recorded, almost perfunctorily, certainly with irony, among the loose ends tied off in the last chapter. That chapter serves the usual purpose of an epilogue in telling readers what happened to characters whose histories are cut short when Edmund breaks with Mary. But Jane Austen makes it serve a second, unusual end. She uses it to take a retrospective look at some of the characters and situations she has imagined, a more coolly reflective look than the impetus of the novel permitted.

She considers alternatives to what she has done. First there is the personality of Fanny herself. As niece-companion to Lady Bertram, Fanny is replaced by her sister Susan, and Susan undergoes none of Fanny's misery and develops none of her shrinking. The reader naturally bears in mind that Susan is 14, not 10, when she arrives, that she has been well prepared by Fanny for what she will meet, that Fanny is there with her, that Maria and Julia (and soon Mrs Norris) are not. But, surprisingly, these obvious explanations are not mentioned; the only reason Jane Austen gives for her easier fate is her different personality:

> Her more fearless disposition and happier nerves made everything easy to her there. – With quickness in understanding the tempers of those she had to deal with, and no natural timidity to restrain any consequent wishes, she was soon welcome, and useful to all.

By implication, that is, Jane Austen recognizes that it was not intrinsic to the situation that Fanny should have been made quite so much the shrinking, creepmouse person who was doomed to be victimized, the crushed heroine who, at least by the time she is 16, brings uncertainty or reservations into the sympathy we are invited to feel.

What is still more remarkable, Jane Austen lets herself consider a totally different upshot of the contact between the Crawfords' values and those of Fanny and Edmund. In the novel itself Jane Austen had clearly presented the difficulties and limitations of marriages with the Crawfords. Mary's reluctance to live in the country on a small income with a socially undistinguished and unambitious husband had been unsparingly displayed. And her firm approval of Henry's marriage to Fanny went with a cool view of its realistic prospects: she tells her brother 'I know that a wife you *loved* would be the happiest of women, and that even when you ceased to love, she would yet find in you the liberality and good-breeding of a gentleman'; to Fanny she says 'If any man ever loved a woman for ever, I think Henry will do as much for you'; and to Edmund, when Henry has gone off with Maria, she laments Fanny's not accepting him because then 'He would have taken no pains to be on terms with Mrs Rushworth again. It would have all ended in a regular standing flirtation, in yearly meetings at Sotherton and Everingham.' These are not the prospects Jane Austen holds out in the marriages that make the happy ending of her novels.

In the novel itself she can say that among Fanny's sources of delight on returning to Mansfield Park were the facts that 'she was safe from Mr Crawford' and above all that 'Edmund was no longer the dupe of Miss Crawford'; and she can vividly convey Edmund's shock and revulsion during their last meeting at the revelation of Mary's moral standards. If Henry had 'done as he intended, and as he knew he ought', by going into Norfolk to ensure the proper treatment of his tenants (instead of being flattered into staying for Mrs Fraser's party and being piqued into overcoming Maria's resentment), 'he might have been deciding his own happy destiny':

> His affection had already done something. Her influence over him had already given him some influence over her. Would he have deserved more, there can be no doubt that more would have been obtained; especially when that marriage had taken place, which would have given him the assistance of her conscience in subduing her first inclination, and brought them very often together. Would he have persevered, and

uprightly, Fanny must have been his reward – and a reward very voluntarily bestowed – within a reasonable period from Edmund's marrying Mary.

Clearly Jane Austen invites us here to feel regret at the lost opportunities, not (as in the body of the novel) to share in Fanny's relief and Edmund's shocked recoil. The inconsistency only brings to the surface undercurrents in the novel itself – the difficulty of finding Fanny attractive as well as worthy and of feeling sure that her merits completely outweigh Mary's friendly charm. By the time we reach the epilogue chapter we have been prepared to share in a regret that there could be no union between the two contrasting pairs – Fanny and Edmund serious and sensitive but rather in need of enlivening, the Drawfords lively and sophisticated while still socially perceptive enough to appreciate Fanny and Edmund in a way totally beyond people like Tom and his sisters or the Honourable John Yates. But the Crawfords' upbringing had suffered from the same deficiency that Sir Thomas at last saw in Maria's and Julia's: 'He feared that principle, active principle, had been wanting, that they had never been properly taught to govern their inclinations and tempers, by that sense of duty which can alone suffice. They had been instructed theoretically in their religion, but never required to bring it into daily practice.'

Their lack of principle made it impossible to unite their good qualities (liveliness, generosity and frankness, social skill and perceptiveness, tact) with the worthier but stodgier cousins. For Edmund the break with Mary is presented as undiluted loss, simple misery. For Fanny, after her first moral shock at the adultery, there was relief, with joy at being once more secure of the adored Edmund, at least as his only 'sister' while she submerged her further yearnings. Early in the novel Jane Austen had called the fraternal tie superior to the conjugal as a 'strengthener of love', a reflection that might seem to cast some coolness on the supreme felicity of the marriage between lovers that should bring the novel to its happy end. In the outcome she united the fraternal and conjugal bonds. With undisguised irony she leaves it to the reader to decide how long it was before Edmund fell in love with the girl whom he had embraced as 'My Fanny – my only sister – my only comfort now.' Mrs Norris's assurance to Sir Thomas when they first considered relieving Mrs Price of the burden of her daughter put the accepted prospect clearly:

> You are thinking of your sons – but do not you know that of all things upon earth *that* is the least likely to happen; brought up, as they would be, always together like brothers and sisters? It is morally impossible.

In the end we are asked to accept the opposite as 'quite natural':

> I only intreat every body to believe that exactly at the time when it was quite natural that it should be so, and not a week earlier, Edmund did cease to care about Miss Crawford, and became as anxious to marry Fanny, as Fanny herself could desire.
>
> With such a regard for her, indeed, as his had long been, a regard founded on the most endearing claims of innocence and helplessness, and completed by every recommendation of growing worth, what could be more natural than the change?

But whether we have been contemplating the fraternal tie or the conjugal tie in the making has been the uncertainty throughout the novel.

Appendix A
The Supposed Letter Form of
Sense and Sensibility

One of the minor curiosities of literature is the stubborn persistence of the story that *Sense and Sensibility* was originally in the form of letters, though nobody can see who the correspondents could have been. B.C. Southam (*Jane Austen's Literary Manuscripts* (1964)) did a valuable service by accepting the story without question but going on to show in detail what difficulties it presented. His serious and determined attempt to overcome them could hardly be improved on, but in the end only reinforces scepticism because it has to rely so much on invention. Additional correspondents for both Elinor and Marianne have to be provided, with no convincing traces of either in the existing text. What is offered as a clue to Elinor's missing confidant clearly refers to Edward Ferrars. And for Marianne it can only be suggested that some of her speeches and musings 'read like passages from the letters of a sentimental heroine' – as of course they are meant to – and 'may have been carried over from her original letters to a confidante at Norland, a girl of matching tempera-ment'. They may. But with such freedom of inventive supposition there are altogether too many novels for which we could surmise an earlier epistolary form.

Southam's willingness to come to grips with the prob-lem, the thoroughness with which he has combed the novel without finding better evidence than he offers, and the frankness with which he has recognized the necessity of inventing eliminated correspondents make it clear that the novel itself would not have suggested an original letter form in the absence of some external evidence.

The adequacy of the external evidence is therefore crucial. In 1870 *A Memoir of Jane Austen* by J.E. Austen-Leigh reported that *Sense and Sensibility* was begun in 1797, adding 'But something similar in story and character had been written earlier under the title of "Elinor and Marianne."' Nothing is said of its being in letter form, though that supposed fact was included in the information that Austen-Leigh had received from his sister Caroline Austen as he prepared the *Memoir*. According to Chapman (*Facts and Problems*, p. 168) he preserved correspondence on the *Memoir* in a volume passed down in the family – 'letters from his sister, his half-sister, and others, written in or about 1869, giving him information or advice'; and Chapman quotes Caroline Austen's own words from her letter:

> Memory is treacherous, but I cannot be mistaken in saying that *Sense and Sensibility* was *first* written in letters, and *so* read to her family.

Why her brother chose to leave out that reminiscence is of course not explained: perhaps he was alerted by the preliminary note of warning; probably he saw that there are no characters between whom the necessary letters could pass; certainly he knew his sister better than we can.

He having omitted the story, the first public reference to the supposed letter form was the statement by his son and grandson (Austen-Leigh, Richard J. and W.) in 1913 (*Life and Letters*, p. 80) that 'To this period [the early years at Chawton] belongs *Elinor and Marianne*, a first sketch for *Sense and Sensibility*, but written in letters.' Southam takes that statement to be corroborated by Caroline Austen's reminiscence. But that almost certainly reverses the sequence. There can be no reasonable doubt that the Austen-Leighs saw her words before they wrote: they say (vi) 'every existing MS, or tradition preserved by the family, of which we have any knowledge, has been placed at our disposal'. And since there is no record of any other evidence for an epistolary version it must have been her letter they relied on, as biographers have done ever since.

'Memory is treacherous.' This kind of initial caution before convincing herself she remembers rightly is not found in *My Aunt Jane Austen*, Caroline Austen's account of Jane Austen and Chawton as she recalled them from her childhood visits; in that record (on which she worked between 1865 and 1867) she was writing spontaneously, not trying, as in 1869, to supply her brother with material for his more extensive and systematic *Memoir*. In *My Aunt Jane Austen* very little is said about the novels, nothing at all about any of them individually. As she was only 12 when Jane Austen died it seems likely, as Southam assumes, that in what she said of *Sense and Sensibility* she was trying to recall grown-up conversation she had listened to. 'Memory is treacherous': how surprisingly treacherous in its omissions, inventions, and distortions was demonstrated by European studies in the psychology of testimony at the end of the nineteenth century and early in the twentieth. But common experience reveals the same facts: there are things involving ourselves that our friends 'remember' in perfectly good faith and we can swear never happened; they have 'forgotten' things we 'remember' about them; and biographers of people who lived recently enough to be remembered by several informants are only too familiar with the difficulty of reconciling different and honestly meant accounts of the same event.

It seems unlikely that Caroline Austen's 'memory' of what she heard about *Sense and Sensibility* was made up out of whole cloth; distortion was probably at work rather than creation. In edition the *Memoir* by J.E. Austen-Leigh (published in the same volume as the Penguin edition of *Persuasion* [1965]) I suggested that it was more likely to have been *Pride and Prejudice* (perhaps under its original title of *First Impressions*) which as a child she heard spoken of as having first been in letter form. Trying after a lapse of more than 50 years to recall what she overheard as a child, she may easily have salvaged from what was said about *Sense and Sensibility* that fact that it was first called *Elinor and Marianne* and then, when the talk moved on to *Pride and Prejudice* or *First Impressions*, that that novel had first been in letter form. Reversing and fusing two such bits of information is most certainly not beyond the resources of 'memory'.

A brief survey or recall of *Pride and Prejudice* shows how easily the narrative could have been conveyed in letters. Some of the most important incidents (at Rosings, Pemberley, and Brighton) occur while Elizabeth and Jane are separated and could have written to each other in complete confidence. And when they are together Elizabeth has in her aunt Mrs Gardiner another correspondent on whose sympathy and discretion she can fully rely even when she criticizes her parents and younger sisters or tells of her feelings about Wickham and Darcy.

Although not certain, it seems likely that letters and fragments of letters will remain fairly prominent when correspondence is converted into ordinary narrative; and without undue fervour for statistics we can still get help from a simple count of letters and parts of letters in the two novels. Two measures are needed:

(a) letter mentions, the total number of letters and notes (even short notes) mentioned in any way, from brief reference to full verbatim presentation
(b) verbatim lines, the number of lines used (fully or partly) to present a letter-writer's words, whether as a complete letter or a quotation from it.

Both measures have to be related to the length of the novel. (I have used Chapman's third edition, 1932 and 1933, for the number of pages and lines.) The numbers are:

Pride and Prejudice
(388 pages): letter mentions 52 (1 to 7 pages);
(14,744 lines): verbatim lines 954 (1 to 15 lines).

Sense and Sensibility
(380 pages): letter mentions 22 (1 to 17 pages);
(14,440 lines): verbatim lines 200 (1 to 72 lines).

With more than twice as many letters or notes mentioned and nearly five times as much verbatim correspondence included, *Pride and Prejudice* looks by far the likelier novel to have started out in letter form. But (tedious or not) the corresponding figures for the other novels must also be noted, in order to see whether *Pride and Prejudice* only, and not *Sense and Sensibility*, differs from novels assumed to have begun as ordinary narrative:

Mansfield Park
(467 pages): letter mentions 49 (1 to 10 pages);
(17,746 lines): lines verbatim 482 (1 to 37 lines).

Emma
(475 pages): letter mentions 53 (1 to 9 pages);
(18,050 lines): lines verbatim 325 (1 to 56 lines).

Northanger Abbey
(237 pages): letter mentions 14 (1 to 17 pages),
(9,006 lines): lines verbatim 121 (1 to 74 lines).

Persuasion
(247 pages): letter mentions 21 (1 to 14 pages);
(9,386 lines): lines verbatim 154 (1 to 61 lines).

Pride and Prejudice mentions more, but not a great many more, notes and letters than *Mansfield Park* or *Emma*, but it uses twice as much verbatim letter material as *Mansfield Park*, nearly four times as much as *Emma*, and in both measures far outdoes *Northanger Abbey* and *Persuasion*. By contrast, *Sense and Sensibility* on these measures is fairly close to *Northanger Abbey* and *Persuasion*, and uses actually *less* letter material than *Mansfield Park* and *Emma*. Nothing here can support the view that it differs from the other novels through retaining vestiges of an original letter form.

While I was preparing my edition of the *Memoir* Southam's book had not appeared or I should have seen that he too believed *Pride and Prejudice* to have been first written as letters (though he still held to the established view about *Sense and Sensibility*). He too assumed that an original letter form will produce an unusually large number of letters and references to letters in the narrative version, and he compared the two novels in this respect. He found that *Pride and Prejudice* had more than twice as many. For him, however, this simply strengthened the likelihood that *Pride and Prejudice* began as letters, since *Sense and Sensibility*, which – he believed – certainly began in that form, retains only half as many. The alternative view would have been that if many passages of correspondence in the one novel argue for an earlier letter form their fewness in the other argues against it. But it is the comparison of each of these with the other novels, especially in their use of correspondents' words verbatim, which puts it beyond doubt that *Pride and Prejudice* stands decisively apart from the rest; and, what is equally important, that *Sense and Sensibility* does not. Memory really is treacherous, and I think Caroline Austen simply made a mistake.

A Note on the Letter Form of *Pride and Prejudice*

The time needed for transforming the letters to the narrative form of *Pride and Prejudice* may have been one contributory reason, in addition to those usually suggested, for Jane Austen's choice of *Sense and Sensibility* as the first novel to appear when she determined seriously on publication. There was much more to be done than the lopping and cropping she spoke of to Cassandra. Many situations could be presented with vastly greater effect in narrative. So, for example, Elizabeth waits until she call tell Jane by word of mouth about Darcy's first proposal and his letter next day, the narrative exploiting the advantage of Jane's interventions and comments. Again, while much of what happened at Pemberley could easily have gone into a letter to Jane the surprise and puzzlement of the Gardiners could much better be put by an omniscient author – who could say, for example, that in returning from the ceremonial visit to Darcy's sister 'They talked of his sister, his friends, his house, his fruit, of everything but himself; yet Elizabeth was longing to know what Mrs Gardiner thought of him, and Mrs Gardiner would have been highly gratified by her niece's beginning the subject.' The deeply moving quality of the interview between Elizabeth and her father when Darcy's proposal bursts on him would have been difficult to express through a letter from Elizabeth herself. It may even be doubted whether the tense episode of Lady Catherine's call at Longbourn and her challenge to Elizabeth in the shrubbery could have been conveyed so well by letter, especially since Elizabeth had not yet told Mrs Gardiner how differently she now felt about Darcy. But at this point the small factual question of the novel's original form begins to merge with the more important concerns of literary enjoyment.

Appendix B
An Introduction to the Austen-Leigh Memoir

A generation removed far enough from the Victorians to feel less of the dislike they engendered in their immediate successors can read J.E. Austen-Leigh's *Memoir* of his aunt with the discrimination it deserves and recognize in it, despite limitations of frankness and understanding, one of those pioneering biographies to which the meticulous search of later scholarship has added only a little. It forms a bridge between her time and the late Victorians and Edwardians, whose view of her and her work it helped to shape. When it was written, just over fifty years after her death, Regency society had gone and with it had gone to a great extent the sense (especially evident in *Mansfield Park* but present in most of Jane Austen's novels) that moral values had to be sustained against the threat of influential example. Society near the Court had turned its official back on vice, and that now belonged to the lower orders whose example had no dangerous gilding. In spite of a personal humility that seems genuine, Austen-Leigh writes with staggering complacency of the material and moral advances his generation had achieved; he tends to assimilate his aunt's work to his contemporaries' outlook rather than point the contrast, and he thus contributed to the idea that her works were all charm and urbane comment on a society in which she felt at ease.

He also offers an idealized view of her life within her family and immediate circle of friends. When he wrote the *Memoir* he was 71 and under strong persuasion from

other members of the family towards reticence and discretion. He followed the family practice of completely
ignoring the existence of her defective or handicapped
brother and he played down her love affairs. Her sister
Cassandra had done much to the same end by her ruthless
destructions and excisions amongst the letters. But the
chief responsibility for this polite conspiracy to idealize
her situation must rest with Jane Austen herself; Cassandra's censorship was in the spirit of her sister's own tact
and gratitude as a poor relation and adored spinster aunt
and the patient daughter of a mother who was constantly
unwell (and lived to be 88). No one who reads the *Memoir*
can doubt that she followed this programme naturally and
well and that it reflected part of her personality. It is
equally evident that the novels would not have been what
they are unless she had at the same time been a very
different person.

The slight pieces of evidence for supplementing
Austen-Leigh's accounts have been scrupulously assembled
and sifted by R.W. Chapman (*Jane Austen: Facts and
Problems*, Oxford, 1948). But there is not a lot to add to
the *Memoir* factually. It is possible to make out that the
developing attachment between her and Tom Lefroy was
more serious and that its breaking in 1796 hurt her more
than Austen-Leigh suggests. In 1798 she evidently
attracted, but apparently was not attracted by, a Mr
Blackall of Emmanuel, who later got a college living and
married someone else. In the summer of 1802, during a
visit to Teignmouth, there occurred the meeting,
described briefly in the *Memoir*, with a man who was so
much attracted by her, and she by him, that Cassandra
thought it would lead to marriage. They were expecting
to see him again but heard from his brother – how soon is
uncertain – that he had died. In the autumn of the same
year she received a proposal. Austen-Leigh's brief reference to the gentleman whose addresses she declined

conceals the more agitated incident of her visit in 1802 to Manydown, an estate near Steventon, where Harris Bigg Wither, the 21-year-old heir, proposed to her (she being about six years older) and was accepted. But the next morning she withdrew her consent, and she and Cassandra returned at once to Steventon, upset but giving no explanation and insisting that their brother, with whom they were staying, should drive them home to Bath next day. In spite of the uncertainties, and the determination of the family to make out that Jane Austen was never seriously unhappy, there is every reason to conclude that in her early and middle 20s she went through the agitations that those years commonly bring, that she experienced disappointment in love and that she refused marriage without it.

Jane Austen's serious creative work emerged gradually from the playful exercises in fiction that she offered for the entertainment of her family. Early versions of *Sense and Sensibility*, *Pride and Prejudice* and *Northanger Abbey* were written between 1796 and 1799. Since even in its final form the last of these is the least mature of her finished novels we can be sure that the other two were very different in their early form from what they became on publication many years later. The story that *Sense and Sensibility* existed first in the form of letters is improbable; it derives solely from a note made at the age of 64 by a niece who was not born until 1805. But she may have heard this said of *Pride and Prejudice*, in which an original letter form can much more plausibly be traced. Jane Austen's father did try in 1797 to get *Pride and Prejudice* (then called *First Impressions*) published, but with no success. There is no record of her writing during the next four years. They included the move to Bath in 1801 (which is thought to have been very unwelcome to her), the abortive romance at Teignmouth and the proposal from Bigg Wither. But in 1803 she put her Bath novel (then called *Susan*, now *Northanger Abbey*) into more finished form and managed with her brother Henry's help to sell it to a publisher – who, however, failed to bring it out in spite of having advertised it. In 1803 or 1804, probably, she was also writing *The Watsons*, a novel that was left unfinished. Her discouraging attempts at publication were followed by her father's death in January 1805; and for the next four years Mrs Austen and her two daughters, with a small income, were living first in lodgings and then in a shared house in Southampton.

Soon after the move to Chawton Cottage was decided on she turned again, and more seriously, to the idea of publication, first trying in 1809 (and without success) to get the purchaser of *Northanger Abbey* to publish it. By 1811, putting aside money to meet the expected loss, she published *Sense and Sensibility* at her own expense, evidently after revision. In the same year she began writing *Mansfield Park*. In 1812 she largely reconstructed *Pride and Prejudice*, which was published in 1813. In the summer of 1813 she finished *Mansfield Park*. *Emma* was written between January 1814 and March 1815, and *Persuasion* between August 1815 and August 1816. In 1816 she also bought back *Northanger Abbey* and revised it for immediate publication (though she shelved it again and had some doubts about its ever appearing). And finally in the early months of 1817 she was at work on *Sanditon*, unfinished when she died.

The usual view, that she had two creative periods – her early twenties and her late thirties – divided by a largely barren interval, seems misleading. The novels as we know them were all produced in the later period. If the early versions, *Elinor and Marianne*, *First Impressions* and *Susan*, had been published, Jane Austen's standing would be lower. Her creative work went through the stages first of a practice period which grew out of a childhood pursuit and provided entertainment for her family and friends (with easily discouraged attempts at publication); second, of a period in which she wrote little but in which new standards may well have been forming; finally of the period from 1809 to her death, when she committed herself with much more determination to authorship for the public, thoroughly reshaped the early family productions and produced new work with remarkable fertility and freshness.

Appendix C
D. W. Harding: A biographical Chronology

Denys Wyatt Clement Harding was born on 13 July **1906**, at Lowestoft in Suffolk, the only son and third child of Harriet and Clement Harding.

He was educated at Lowestoft Secondary School.

In **1920** his father, Clement Harding, died.

In **1925** he entered Emmanuel College, Cambridge, where he subsequently won an Exhibition and became (in 1927) a Senior Scholar. He read English Literature and Psychology.

He obtained his B.A. (with a double First) in **1928**.

From **1928** to **1933** he worked for the NIIP (National Institute of Industrial Psychology) as a member of the research staff.

In **1930** he married Jessie Muriel Ward whom he had known since his schooldays. They had no children.

He was invited to join the editorial board of *Scrutiny* in **1933**. He served on the board until **1947**.

In **1933** he was also appointed as a Lecturer in Social Psychology at the London School of Economics.

His mother, Harriet Harding, died in **1936**.

In the same year he translated (with Eric Mesterton) *Guest of Reality* by Par Lagerkvist.

In **1938** he edited (with Gordon Bottomley) *The Complete Works of Isaac Rosenberg*.

In **1938** he was appointed to a Senior Lectureship in Psychology at Manchester University; he held this post until 1945, but was on war service from **1941** to **1944**.

In **1941** his first book, *The Impulse to Dominate*, was published. The bulk of the print run of this book was destroyed in a warehouse fire during the Blitz. Because of war-time paper restrictions it was never reprinted.

In the years before and after his war service, he also had a part-time Lectureship at Liverpool University.

In **1944** he became the Honorary General Secretary of The British Psychological Society, an office he held until **1948**.

In **1945** he was appointed Professor of Psychology in the University of London, the Chair being held at Bedford College.

Between **1948** and **1954** he was editor of *The British Journal of Psychology* (General Section).

In **1947** he and his wife Jessie bought the Old Vicarage at Ashbocking, in Suffolk, where they lived for the rest of their lives.

His second book, *Social Psychology and Individual Values*, was published in **1953**.

In **1963** *Experience Into Words: Essays and Poetry* was published.

During the **1960**s he made a number of overseas visits and lecture tours to the USA, India, Hong Kong, New Zealand and South Africa. The subject-matter of the lectures on some of these visits was, in the main, psychology, but others were largely, or solely, concerned with literary criticism.

In **1968** he retired, resigning his Chair at Bedford College a few years early.

During the academic year **1971/72** he held the Clark Lectureship at Trinity College, Cambridge; the substance of those lectures was published in his last book, *Words into Rhythm* (**1976**).

In **1991** his wife Jessie died after a long illness.

On 21st April **1993** of D.W. Harding died in his 87th year.

Notes

Chapter 1

A paper read before the Literary Society of Manchester University in March 1939. Published in *Scrutiny* VIII (1940), pp. 346–62.

Chapter 2 and 3

Prepared from the manuscripts of several unpublished lectures; probably prepared and delivered in the 1960s or 1970s. Some overlapping and duplicate material has been removed by the editor.

Chapter 4

Part of an essay entitled 'The character of Literature from Blake to Byron' published in the book of that name edited by Boris Ford and published by Penguin, Harmondsworth (1957).

Chapter 5

Published in *Critical Essays on Jane Austen*, ed. B.C. Southam, Routledge & Kegan Paul, London (1968).

Chapter 61

This was originally prepared as a lecture and, probably, delivered during the 1970s. In the case of this essay some detailed notes are required because of the references to other critical work.

6/1 T. Tanner, Southam, ed., p. 138.

6/2 See addendum to Chapter 1.

6/3 Southam, B.C. *A Student's Guide to the Selected Poems of T.S. Eliot* (1968).

6/4 W. Porter Ware & Thaddeus C. Lockhard Jr. (eds), *The Lost Letters of Jenny Lind*, London (1966).

6/5 Chapman, R.W. *Jane Austen: Facts and Problems*, Oxford (1948), p. 17.

Chapter 7

A much revised manuscript which had not been published because the author thought it in need of further revision. The date is uncertain, but it existed in some form by 1980.

Chapter 8

Published as an Introduction the edition of Jane Austen's *'Persuasion' with a memoir of Jane Austen by J.E. Austen Leigh* (which he edited) in the Penguin Library Series, Penguin, Harmondsworth (1965).

Chapter 9

Prepared in its present form between 1987 and 1993, may have been based on an earlier lecture. Unpublished.

Chapter 10

Unpublished. Evidently written about 1991/92; described on the pcw disc from which it has been copied as a 'rough draft'.

Appendix A

Written after 1990, in press at the time of the author's death. Published in *Notes and Queries*, Vol. 238, pp. 464–6, December 1993.

Appendix B

An introduction from the Austen Leigh memoir, published in the Penguin edition of *Persuasion* referred to in the note on Chapter 8 (above).

Index